KEEPING OUR TROTH

BY THE AUTHOR

I Pledge You My Troth

KEEPING OUR TROTH

Staying in Love Through the Five Stages of Marriage

JAMES H. OLTHUIS

1817

Harper & Row, Publishers, San Francisco

Cambridge, Hagerstown, New York, Philadelphia, Washington
London, Mexico City, São Paulo, Singapore, Sydney

Grateful acknowledgement is made for use of the following:

The lines from "On the Streets, Love" are reprinted by permission from *The Circle Game* by Margaret Atwood [Toronto: House of Anansi Press, 1967].

From "Sexual Intelligence," lyrics by Lorraine Segato, Billy Bryans, and Lynne Fernie of the Canadian group, The Parachute Club. Reprinted by permission of Current Sounds, a Division of the Current Entertainment Corporation.

The case histories and examples in this book describe actual situations, although names and identifying details about each person have been changed.

KEEPING OUR TROTH: *Staying in Love Through the Five Stages of Marriage.* Copyright © 1986 by James H. Olthuis. All rights reserved. Printed in the United States of America. No part of this book may be used or reproduced in any manner whatsoever without written permission except in the case of brief quotations embodied in critical articles and reviews. For information address Harper & Row, Publishers, Inc., 10 East 53rd Street, New York, NY 10022. Published simultaneously in Canada by Fitzhenry & Whiteside, Limited, Toronto.

FIRST EDITION

Library of Congress Cataloging-in-Publication Data

Olthuis, James H.
  Keeping our troth.

  Bibliography: p.
  1. Marriage.   2. Interpersonal relations.
3. Marriage—Religious aspects.   I. Title.
HQ734.O59   1986   306.8'1   85-45721
ISBN 0-06-066389-8

86 87 88 89 90   HC   10 9 8 7 6 5 4 3 2 1

To Douglas John, Anita Jolanda, and Christine Janet
In hope and with love

Contents

Preface   ix

1. Intimacy: A Perilous Journey   1
2. Identity and Intimacy   20
3. Stage One: Romance   49
4. Stage Two: Power Struggle   59
5. Stage Three: Shifting Gears   89
6. Stage Four: Mutuality   105
7. Stage Five: Co-Creativity   128
8. The Ongoing Journey   141

Notes   153
Selected Bibliography   156

Preface

Three truths about marriage are carving themselves deeply into our communal consciousness as the twentieth century comes to a close. In this era of anxiety and broken illusions, we know that marriage will survive, even if its forms will be somewhat changed. However, we have also learned that happiness is not a gift that comes prepackaged with marriage, to be consumed in bite-sized pieces. Finally, we are realizing that marriage is a passage with stages, a struggle and a journey toward deeper joy and fulfillment.

Although this book is about all three truths, its focus is on the third. The marriage voyage need not be a trip into the unknown. I hope to dispel some of the mists of illusion and the fogs of myth that settle in and befuddle many couples. I wish to provide a compass and a chart of the marriage course, with its hidden rocks, lurking monsters, shimmering sandbars, and strong gales. With proper preparations and a good map, marriage can be a fulfilling and rewarding adventure even in these tempestuous times.

It remains true, of course, that each and every marriage craft sails out to sea in its own way, from its own port and heading for its own destination. It makes its own reckonings, deals with its own particular weather, navigates its own course, and establishes its own rhythms and routines. Such is the excitement and adventure of each new sailing. However, since all the journeys are on the Seas of Marriage, infamous for their sudden squalls, dark waters, and perilous shores, charts and maps prove invaluable. So easily we strand on the sandbars or crash on the rocks. Even when we sail by the true north of committed troth, ignoring charts is foolhardy. We have to know where the dangerous shoals are to negotiate them safely. The perils and vicissitudes of the Seas of Marriage play no favorites.

Today the shores are strewn with marital wreckage, and prognostications give each marriage about a fifty percent chance of survival. Today, more than ever, we need a map. Not that the map I draw is perfect; no doubt it is incomplete and perhaps even misleading in some places. But it has proven its value as a guide, a description of the trouble spots and an itinerary of the stops along the way.

A successful journey begins with adequate preparations. After an introductory chapter about the obstacles to intimacy and the nature of troth, we turn to the complex interaction between self-identity—intimacy with self—and intimacy with another. Chapters 3 through 7 outline the five stages of marriage. A last chapter encourages all of us to seek help and describes the process of finding support and healing in our journey.

This book aims to help us locate where we are and where we have been in our intimate relations, so that we can place our struggles in context and make sense of them. I hope it will help us to gain an increased awareness of how we arrived at our present situation and a deepened understanding of steps we may take to make our relationship more wholesome and more fulfilling. We will be encouraged to learn new ways of being together that avoid triggering the old, unhelpful responses. I hope that all of us will gain the sense of empowerment that flows from the realization that growth in our sense of self is at the same time the best guarantee for deepened intimacy with another person.

My 1975 book *I Pledge You My Troth* talked about the nature of marriage (as well as family and friendship) from a Christian perspective. Since then in my own marriage, in conducting workshops and retreats, and in counseling couples and individuals, I have seen and experienced how difficult it is for us to live out what we deeply believe. *Keeping Our Troth* is the sequel that has grown out of that experience. What I believe about marriage has not changed, but what has grown is the insight that the struggle to keep the troth in the complexities of life is itself our way of staying committed to God as well as a route to a deepened inner experience of God. Falling in love and pledging troth is a first step; the second, more difficult step is staying in love and keeping troth. The theme of what follows is this second step; keeping troth through the trials and turns of the marriage passage.

There are many people I wish to thank. I owe a debt of gratitude to those who have shared with me, shared their lives, struggles, and joys. To share in a deep way with people is a beautiful gift and a sacred trust—like being on sacred ground, no shoes permitted. I want to thank the Institute for Christian Studies for providing me with the time and support necessary for writing this book. I want to acknowledge and thank the community of people associated with the Bioenergetic Psychotherapy Institute in Toronto for their teaching and support. My thanks and deep appreciation go to friends and colleagues who offered help and suggestions along the way, especially to Diane Marshall, Hendrik Hart, and Arnold De Graaff. My special thanks to Pat Weaver, who so enthusiastically and ably served as editor. And how do I thank Jean, my partner in troth for over twenty-five years? Words are not enough. This book is in a deep sense as much hers as it is mine, because it was conceived, born, and nourished in our journey together.

1. Intimacy: A Perilous Journey

On the streets
love
these days
is a matter for
either scavengers
(turning death to life) or
(turning life
to death) for predators . . .

—MARGARET ATWOOD

Some thirty years ago George Orwell wrote a book that has haunted the Western world ever since. In grim detail, he depicted life in a thought-controlled totalitarian English society of the "future"—*1984*. Out of some 137 specific predictions that Orwell made, over 100 have already come true. He foretold three superpowers waging wars of limited intent in Africa, the Middle East, and Asia; he spoke of defoliants, data banks, artificial insemination, drug-controlled behavior, subcortical surgery, voice analyzers, and on and on. But one of his most chilling predictions has yet to come true—that the family will become obsolescent and the emotional bonds between parents and children will dissolve.

Will it come true? Many social scientists have warned us that marriage and the family are disintegrating and may not survive the century. Many have predicted that the new sexual freedom that permits "instant intimacy" with a long series of partners will win out over the "dullness" of a monogamous marriage and even that well-developed love affairs will become old-fashioned.

But actions speak louder than words. We continue to be preoccupied with finding a single satisfying and intimate relationship: the predictions about the death of love and marriage have been not just premature, but grossly exaggerated, just as were the reports about the death of God. It is true that the percentage of divorces continues to rise, to fifty percent and beyond. Yet it is also true that four out of five divorced persons eventually remarry. Recent statistics reveal a striking increase in the number of unattached individuals, but people in this category include the divorced, widowed, eager-to-get-married, and officially-single-but-involved, as well as those committed to remaining single. The last group seems relatively small. The problem with being unattached is exactly that; it means lacking a deep and lasting connection with another, missing the feeling of mutual belonging, in a word, loneliness. The greatest need single people feel is for a human relationship that provides the basic satisfactions of intimacy, sharing, and companionship.

This kind of closeness and connection is most likely to become a reality within the bounds of mutual commitment. When all is said and done, we humans always long for a deep and special relationship offering warmth, understanding, closeness, and mutuality. More than a Midas touch in the marketplace, more than the respect of peers, more than the approval of parents or teachers we desire the love and intimacy of an ultimate human connection. As long as that remains true, marriage endures. In our society, marriage, with all its pitfalls, still offers the best chance to find the solace and belonging we desire. Tried and true friendships can also give us deep satisfaction, but in our mobile culture such friendships seem even more rare than good marriages.

Marriage is here to stay. But that does not mean marriage is untroubled. The North American divorce rate has risen seven hundred percent in the last hundred years. Today, one out of every two marriages ends in divorce. The bitter reality of the attempt at intimate connection for most of us, married or divorced, living with someone or involved with a series of partners, is echoed in what Albert Schweitzer once said: "We are all so much together, but we are dying of loneliness." For many of us who marry, marriage has not meant the ultimate connection; it has only made us feel more keenly our lack of connection. Marriage has shattered our dreams of belonging somewhere. As our commitments splinter we move toward despair and our hearts grow cold and heavy, weighed down with alienation and distrust.

How can we learn to experience marriage as a meeting-in-the-middle rather than as a tug-of-war? Can there be intimate wedlock rather than holy deadlock? How can our marriages be more like safety islands of support and warmth and less like fur-lined bear traps?

To begin with, we need a sane sense of where we are at. We need to be made aware of and acknowledge the hazards threatening the journey to intimacy. They are many and formidable.

THINGS FIRST, PEOPLE SECOND

We live in a "things-first, people-second" society, which makes genuine love difficult. Instead of being taught to love people and use things, we are more often taught to love things and use people. Such a climate provides precious little room for sharing, caring, and being oneself. We are a society "on the move," ready at a moment's notice to go wherever the technostructure sends us (doesn't IBM stand for "I've Been Moved"?).

Everyone seems to acknowledge that material abundance neither promotes tranquility of spirit nor guarantees happiness—but daily life gives the lie to our words. The incessant message of our third parent, television, is simple and crass: happiness is the accumulation of more and more things. The use-and-dispose-of habit becomes second nature to us and gets used in human relations too. When problems arise, when contacts disappoint, we move on. Our worth is weighed out in money and the goods money buys. Where money and sexual prowess are gods, people become objects to be used and our relationships suffer.

In this climate of consumer self-indulgence, is it any wonder that people draw further and further away from each other as they become more and more attached to things? This distancing makes us think we are "complete" in ourselves, and then other persons, just like things, become accoutrements to be traded in when fashions dictate. In this world, if we open our hearts in commitment and trust to another person, it can often seem that we are only asking to be hurt. The daily soap opera diet teaches us that the only thing we can count on is that some schemer will break up our marriage.

Many of us become too callous, finally, to feel compassion and love. We are left with only sensation and self-pity. Getting deeply involved with another person is not worth the trouble when we will soon be moving on again. A common interest in survival or in climbing the social ladder is what draws us together, at least for the moment.

None of this means that we like to be alone. We need others to assure us that the sensation is worth having, or so we will have someone to "buy off" or be "purchased" by. We need an anonymous crowd to achieve a thin sense of identity. We become desperate to be where the action is, to do what the right people do, to submerge ourselves in our culture—all in futile efforts to find meaning and fulfillment. Little do we know that egotism banishes compassion and our blind hurry destroys any chance of intimacy.

Instead of being a heart-to-heart meeting of persons, what passes for intimacy is all too often a success object relating to a sex object. Instead of the letting-be, giving, and receiving of love, there are the maneuvers of manipulation and alienation. No wonder Jean Paul Sartre said, "Man is born and dies alone and it is only by deluding himself, between these two cardinal events, that he can believe that he is not alone."

THE LADDER OF SUCCESS

The things-first, people-second syndrome is not the only threat to intimacy in our society; there is also its hierarchical and competitive setup. Competition, whether ruthless or civil, seems to be the order of the day. To make it big or even to survive seems to mean taking advantage of others. The dominant cultural image is the ladder of success rather than the circle of mutuality. Getting to the top is what matters. There's a crowd behind waiting for you to falter, waiting to pass you by, so think only of yourself. If your conscience winces, remember, once on top, you'll have so much to share with the less fortunate. Think of all the good you can do—once you have made it.

Fortunately more and more people are calling for change. But the point is that when we are socialized by the dominant cultural values, we see ourselves as competitors ranked on a ladder scale, and our relations are either upward (we take orders) or downward (we give orders). The problem is that distrust and anxiety are built into ladder climbing. The higher we go, the harder we can fall; and to keep ourselves up there we need both hands to hold on—we simply *cannot* reach out to others. Unfortunately, the doctrine of the survival of the fittest, with its individualism and implicit elitism, is still sacralized and stamped with "divine" approval in our society at large. In fact, the word "hierarchy" does not come from the word "higher" but from the word for "sacred." Matthew Fox draws a telling contrast between the elitist, combative, restrictive ladder motif on which the West remains dependent and a welcoming, compassionate, nonviolent circle motif.[1] As long as we remain bewitched by the ladder symbol, the "exile of compassion"—and intimacy—will continue. Isolated, competing egos do not easily open their hearts to each other; caring and sharing in the mutuality of marriage, family, and friendship is at a premium.

Perhaps the saddest thing about our competitive, hierarchical culture is that we don't start out that way. We don't begin life wanting to put others down, but most of us are conditioned from early childhood to accept the harsh realities of life. We become unwilling, compromised, and resigned victims to what we have come to accept as the inevitable. What can we do but play our part?

The hierarchical model has in a special way hurt women. Males, by virtue of being male, have been considered superior to females. God, males, females, children, animals—that's how the order goes. The assumed superiority of males makes the partnership intimacy of marriage difficult. How can you be intimate with a superior without latent feelings of hostility or with an inferior without hidden expectations of being served?

Paradoxically (and this reveals the fallacy of male superiority), males have traditionally not only looked down on females as vessels of lust but have also looked up to females as objects of adoration or as witches to be feared. But this stereotypical mentality does not allow women to be women, equal partners with males in the bi-unity of being human that God created. And neither does it allow men to be men. For men, according to God's intention, are human only in reciprocal relation and mutual interdependence with women. The male-dominant patriarchal marriage, long condoned by church and society, easily becomes an institution to keep women "in their place" rather than a union of mutual affirmation and support. Too often marriage has been an institution that robs both women and men of their humanity.

SEXUAL OBSESSION

A third obstacle to healthy interpersonal relations is our culture's obsession with genital sexuality. Not only have we confused the commitment of love with romantic emotion, we have further confused romance with genital sex. This obsession is related to our culture's priorities: production, consumption, competition, and profit. When the person–thing relationship usurps the person–person relationship, acts of intimacy between people are replaced by acts of intimacy between persons and things: a woman and her car, a cowboy and his horse, a teenager and her jeans, a male and his centerfold. Game shows preview a prize with a sensuous woman stroking it and holding it close to her face, as if the object was part of her own body. Monosexuality or autosexuality has become a way of life, even within the context of hetero- or homosexuality. We so easily treat our partners as objects to be used for our enjoyment.

In our society, persons, especially women, are judged by form and face. But a woman's personal wholeness is violated when she is reduced to a womb and breasts. In reaction, women use their charms as weapons to beguile, dominate, and even destroy men. When a partner no longer titillates or when the conquest is made, the relationship loses its allure. Instead of mutual bonds of intimacy, relationships become helter-skelter contacts or contracts for mutual exploitation.

Our modern obsession with genital sexuality has been encouraged by the pernicious myth that being close must lead to the bedroom. In a society such as ours, which seems to give place to physical touch only in sexual embrace (and in the backslapping of athletic conquests), many people can be frantically preoccupied with sex when, in fact, what they deeply need is tactile contact. People develop a deep, desperate skin hunger, especially if they were deprived of adequate holding and cuddling in infancy. They don't want sex so much as to be held and accepted. In large measure our fear of a sexual interpretation has banished kisses, tears, and tenderness from every place except the bedroom. In the human community, their absence is even stranger than their presence.

When we isolate physical, genital sexuality from its rightful place in personal human contact, it becomes a god we serve by concentrating on getting bigger and better orgasms. We become driven by the demon of sex even as we seek the goddess of sex, and then there is nothing human about sex at all.

MARRIAGE STANDS ON ITS OWN

Living in a society where intimacy and vulnerability are exiled to marriage, family, and friendship, we have staggering expectations for these relationships. Yet marriage is no longer as firmly embedded in the social and economic fabric of society as it once was. Considerations of money, class, religion, family, clan, security, and access to a legitimate sexual partner, do not play the momentous role in keeping marriages together that they once did. Today marriage survival is much more dependent on the quality of its intimacy and troth than ever before. Since marriage is no longer the practical and societal necessity it was in times past, when our expectations of intimacy are not met with the intensity we desire, we can decide to leave, and more and more of us are making that decision. And the isolation of the nuclear family often far from the extended family increases the demands on the family unit to provide all intimacy needs. Deep friendships are also increasingly difficult to form and maintain because of the rapid pace of life and the disquieting experience of moving on every two or three years.

THE MYTH OF ROMANTIC LOVE

The myth of romantic love has bedeviled marriages since the eighteenth century. Love and marriage, we say, go together like a horse and carriage. Even though we know better, we still find ourselves dreaming of "falling in love" and "living happily ever after." We long for the gift of one endless and total union. And we still raise our children on "Snow White," "Cinderella," "Sleep ing Beauty," and similar fairy tales. The unsaid lines of each story are the same: "love always triumphs" and "someday this may happen to you." And for women there is a double whammy. "Sleeping Beauty" says it all: "love's first kiss will wake you up." Women, the myth goes, only come alive when Prince Charming arrives.

In the modern scene, movies and soap operas serve up adultery, deception, and discovery as the main fare, but the myth continues unabated, albeit revised. Next time around it (love forever!) may happen to you. Or it (lovesickness, heart palpitations, blushing, faltering voice, faintness, pallor, and erratic eye movements—the symptoms listed twenty-five centuries ago by Sappho) may not last forever with one person, but don't worry, it can be yours with a series of lovers; just be open and ready when it comes.

The myth of romantic love continues to play such a beguiling role in our lives because it trades on our deeply rooted need for intimacy. We dread loneliness. In the end that explains why, despite all the debunking of and the distress in marriage, so many of us nevertheless marry . . . and remarry. We all yearn for the warmth generated by two people who are deeply connected.

SEXUAL STEREOTYPING

Another major obstacle to intimacy is the sexual stereotyping that permeates our society. From birth on boys and girls are told in countless ways what behavior is expected of them as a boy or a girl. We bounce boy babies robustly on our knees and cuddle girl babies protectively as we admire their beauty, in the process encouraging the boys to be active, aggressive, and brave and encouraging the girls to be docile, fragile, and sweet. In children's literature we still see boys helping their dads wash the car or mow the lawn while girls stand by or help mom bring the "men" refreshments. Children grow up learning that it is more appropriate for men to be doctors, lawyers, presidents, carpenters, symphony conductors, pilots, and captains. It is assumed that women more appropriately become nurses, secretaries, homemakers, social workers, teachers, clerks, and waitresses.

These societal stereotypes are slowly breaking down. Yet we are just beginning to understand that our socialization process not only dictates gender-related ways of behavior but shapes central aspects of our inner selves. Men have been socialized to be separate and independent doers; women have been socialized to be connected and dependent nurturers.[2] In the process of attempting to maintain their independence, men learn to keep themselves well defended against their dependency needs, signs of "weakness." To maintain their feeling of connectedness, women learn to take care of others' needs and their own identity needs are seen as "selfishness." The sad result—the dimensions of which are just beginning to emerge—is that men and women *both fear intimacy*. A man has difficulty maintaining a connection and sharing his inner self for fear of being engulfed and smothered. A woman has difficulty separating and sharing her inner self, fearing that her already weak self will be invaded and lost.

Lillian Rubin has recently argued that these deep differences between men and women in our society are not God-given, but are the result of the social fact that a woman is virtually always the primary caregiver during infancy in combination with the reality of our infantile dependence.[3] Of course, the process of stereotyping men and women does not take place overnight. It's a gradual affair that begins at birth and takes hold as it is continually reinforced over time. And the process doesn't work perfectly because boys and men do experience times in which they feel connected and accepted in their own right and because girls and women do experience times in which they feel their own identity even in connection with others. And the process doesn't work perfectly because it does injustice to human nature, which God created as a partnership of male and female identities-in-intimacy.

We can all be thankful that the picture is not as black and white as briefly sketched; there are many different shades of grey. But as long as we continue to insist that it is male to be independent and separate and it is female to be connected and dependent, we will continue to raise a preponderance of men and women who fear the intimacy they yearn for so strongly. Most women who come for therapy complain sadly and sometimes bitterly that their men do not share their inner selves and seem unable to do so. And the men who enter therapy often come bewildered and angry because their wives never seem satisfied. What do women want?

TOO LITTLE SENSE OF SELF

Men and women both want to be close, but we are afraid to be close. Often, we take one step forward and reach out, only to take two steps backward when someone approaches. Meeting in the middle is our deepest and fondest desire, yet we so often retreat. When approached, we sometimes fear invasion, sometimes dependency or commitment, sometimes humiliation and rejection. But always there is fear.

The deepest fears arise from a vague knowledge that we are unsure of ourselves. We lack a solid sense of who we really are. Too little sense of self is at base the major hazard to intimacy. If we don't really know ourselves or trust ourselves, how can we really entrust ourselves to another? Sensing our own fickleness, how can we believe that others will accept us? Fearing emptiness and helplessness, we close down and put up protective walls, shut ourselves off from others. Walls protect, but they are also barriers that cut us off from ourselves and from reaching out to others from the heart.

Mistrustful of myself and others, I need to remain well defended. You will see only my public self. I will keep you at arm's length, for then, at least, I won't get deeply hurt. No wonder that cynicism is so pervasive in the twentieth century. We make a truce with life, aiming for peaceful coexistence with a minimum of pain. If such arrangements are not deeply satisfying and reaffirming, they are at least relatively safe.

The internal conflict we all experience between wanting and fearing closeness and the defensive postures we adopt as we attempt to resolve our ambivalence are dramatically and radically illustrated in marriage. As long as we mistrust ourselves and lack a sense of self-identity, we will be underinvested in our marriage, keeping our real self walled off, or we will be overinvested in our marriage, seeking in marriage our self-identity. In either case, genuine intimacy will remain out of reach.

SURPRISED BY INTIMACY

Now that we have looked at some of the obstacles to intimacy in our culture, we may feel overwhelmed. How on earth can we live lives of love to God and neighbor in such a society? The predicament of being a twentieth-century human comes home to roost. We discover our own complicity in some of the worst dimensions of our society. We too resist lowering our standard of living so that all the people of the world may have their rightful share of the earth's resources. We feel powerless to effect change in society. We discover the seeds of racism and sexism in ourselves. We begin to feel our own fear of closeness. We don't want to be used and exploited, yet we find ourselves using and exploiting others. We know what it means to escape from ourselves and from others in obsessions with sex, power, or money. We find ourselves trapped by our fear of failure—failure by our culture's standards of success. Underneath, we want to be accepted and loved not for our doing, but for our being; yet we too get lost in our doing. One can hardly exaggerate the difficulty of living a wholesome life in an unhealthy society. The journey of intimacy seems to wind through a minefield; at every step there's disaster. Family, marriage, and friendship—God-given routes to intimacy—even often become, in a phrase of Jules Henry, "pathways to madness."

Yet to care deeply about the needs of persons, to acknowledge the right of animals, to fight for stewardly use of the world's physical resources—to be compassionate as God in heaven is compassionate—is a cardinal mark of being human. Personhood, compassion, and commitment are what God wants for us. For we are copartners with God, called to love and service. The Good News is that in the Spirit of Jesus we can be released to lives of mercy, justice, and intimacy. After all, intimacy, not alienation, is the fundamental truth of the universe.

Release takes a change of heart, a new set of priorities, a reordering of societal structures. A life of liberty takes work, inner

and outer, alone and in concert with others. If the battle for
intimacy is to be won, there needs to be change on every front.
On the broader front, sharing and caring rather than taking and
demanding need to become hallmarks of our culture. We need
to recover a sense of the community of humankind and a sense
of solidarity with all nonhuman forms of life. The circle of compassion must preempt the elitist and competitive ladder of
success.

Fundamental changes in our societal structures are a necessary
part of recovering intimacy. At the same time, growth in self-
esteem and the experience of intimacy in the personal worlds of
marriage, family, friendship, and the community of faith will
free us to take the risks necessary to bring about change and
combat injustice in the world at large. Personal growth and societal renewal belong together. We can't have one without the
other.[4]

TROTH: COMMITTED TRUST

In our effort to achieve a deeper level of intimacy in marriage,
commitment plays a crucial role. In marriage the partners exchange pledges of troth. Two people commit themselves to journey together, sharing and enriching each other in love. Marriage
is the ultimate human connection, a one-flesh union of pledged
troth between two people. Genital sex is an important ingredient
of being one flesh—eros as the drive to union and source of
tenderness is equally indispensable to marriage—but the mutual
commitment of troth is the bond that makes a marriage a marriage. Troth is the key. Troth without eros and sexual union is
thin, burdensome, and unexciting. Eros and sex without troth is
capricious and fleeting.

To betroth oneself is to commit oneself to another person, to
promise loyalty, devotion, nurture, trust, and care.[5] Mutual be-
trothal is the conjoining of persons who embark on a journey of
togetherness, wholeness, respect, tolerance, and love. Marriage
is a mutual affair, a two-way relation in which the members of
a couple commit themselves to a sharing and nurturing way of
being in the world, a way of being that includes not only themselves, but all people, creatures, and God. Taking turns leading

and following in accord with gifts, opportunities, and needs, partners commit themselves to a process of deepening their troth and expanding their intimacy.

The mutual commitment of troth is crucial throughout the stages and phases of the process because it answers the question of loyalty and trust. Troth means that we are fully committed to each other; we promise to respect and support each other as persons in our shared life-style and shared commitments. If this remains unclear, the question of commitment comes to haunt the relationship at every turn. Any disagreement or difference may raise fears that the partner wants out. One partner's time of solitude may be interpreted as a withdrawal and selfishness by the other. Without mutual troth, the partners lack the confidence for complete and open sharing. We begin to hold parts of ourselves back, edgy and fretful that we will not be affirmed and accepted.

However, when the commitment to share and grow together is clear and unreserved, we are encouraged freely and openly to share with each other our inner struggles and doubts as well as our joys and triumphs. The little frictions and larger skirmishes that are part of the journey can be what they are rather than escalate into endless rehearsals of the central issue: do you really accept me? Are you really committed to me as the person I am with all my ways of being, including my anxieties, strengths, and weaknesses? When flare-ups or freeze-outs occur, they do not need to jeopardize the basic relationship; they can be shared and explored. In the doldrums of missed connections and in the storms we all go through because of pressures in our lives or earlier hurts and old patterns, our mutual troth gives us the freedom and space to work on the problem areas together. Without such shared trust, our relationship drifts without direction.

Although the essential commitment to a fulfilling and satisfying marriage is there, sometimes unfulfilling and destructive emotional dovetailing makes it impossible for genuine intimacy to be experienced. Particularly when problems remain unacknowledged for years and years or when the partners remain stuck in certain defensive postures, unable to own their parts in the relationship, the commitment, no matter how genuine at the outset, may gradually erode and disappear. At the same time, when we experience deep connection with each other, when we feel received and affirmed, it becomes safer to be vulnerable. We begin to risk more of ourselves from deeper and deeper layers of our personalities. And our commitment deepens and grows.

TROTH: THE JOURNEY IN FIVE STAGES

Shared troth is not a static entity, not a treasure we can take out on occasion and admire. It is an everchanging gift we spontaneously and freely continue to give and receive. Two people in troth commit themselves to a process of making their relationship safer and safer so that they can open up more intimately to each other.

The process of intimacy appears to follow a sequence with recognizable stages and phases, each with its own unique calling, opportunity, and dynamic. A new stage of intimacy becomes a reality when the ongoing changes combine to create a significant change in the relationship as a whole, giving rise to a new level of functioning and a more complex pattern of integration with new demands, capacities, expectations, and dangers. At the same time, it is well to keep in mind that in reality the movement from stage to stage is usually more gradual and less clear-cut than the descriptions suggest.

Following Erik Erikson's pioneering work on psychosocial development, I suggest that at each stage of the passage there is a main calling or set of tasks that the couple must especially attend to at that stage. A particular set of tasks comes to special prominence during a certain stage, creates its own unique opportunities, and needs to be resolved in one way or another during that critical period. Later stages build on earlier ones, and earlier ones point to later ones. If a calling is not satisfactorily resolved during its period of ascendancy, the relationship as a whole is arrested, broken, or adversely affected—even if the couple remains together. The relationship is conflicted: it needs to move on but is not ready to move on. When the couple experiences new strength and healing, then new possibilities break the deadlocked relationship and move it on toward deepened intimacy.

In this book the journey of intimacy is described in five stages.[6]

STAGE	CALLING	DANGER
1. ROMANCE	grounding in reality	ungrounding
2. POWER STRUGGLE	adjusting to differences	competing, projecting
3. SHIFTING GEARS	renegotiating	retrenching
4. MUTUALITY	connecting	retreating, idling
5. CO-CREATIVITY	interconnecting	scattering

When we talk of a stage, we are talking about a general pattern that characterizes the relationship as a whole at that juncture. The name chosen to describe that stage highlights its strongest feature. The fact that the first stage is called Romance and the second stage is called Power Struggle does not mean that romance doesn't occur or is out of place in any other stage or that power struggles are not part of any other stage. What we mean is that romance captures the flavor of the initial stage just as power struggle typifies Stage Two.

The callings are not limited to certain stages. Thus, romance, renewed and reworked, will show up in all the later stages, and power struggles, shifting gears, mutuality, and co-creativity will be present in some form during Romance. Co-creativity will, likewise, play its own role in the earlier stages, even as struggle will not be absent during Co-Creativity. However, it remains true that at each stage one task comes to the fore with special urgency, the resolution of which is crucial for moving on to a deeper stage of intimacy.

Although the five stages follow in linear sequence, there is no guarantee that every committed relationship will in fact pass through all of them. Some relationships stall in Stage Two until one of the partners or the marriage dies. And the length of a marriage is not necessarily a good sign of the health of a marriage—other than showing that the partners have stuck it out together.

These five stages of marital troth have gone generally unnoticed. Why? Because changes in marriage have so much to do with personal changes, with intertwinement between marriage and family relations, on the one hand, and with societal contexts, on the other. For many the stages of marriage are hardly distinguishable from stages of the family. They talk of courtship, marriage, childbirth, middle marriage, children leaving home, retirement, and old age. Others refer to couple formation, families with young children, families with adolescent children, and families with grown children. However, we gain much by understanding that the ongoing troth relationship between husband and wife has its own intrinsic dynamic. We gain even more by paying explicit attention to this dynamic, particularly in our culture in which marriage has largely lost its traditional supports of providing economic security and social status and now stands or falls with troth alone.

Although the stages of marriage have their own integrity, we need to acknowledge the rich diversity and complex interconnection that marriages enjoy in society. Our intimate journeys will be influenced by differences in class, race, ethnic groups, socialization, vocation, children, education, wealth, beliefs, mores, health, and all the other features of our personal and societal contexts. Thus, the quality of marital intimacy will be affected, for example, by the needs and demands of growing young children. Economic insecurity and unemployment can so galvanize our concerns that there is little time for intimacy. And if progeny rather than intimacy is the major concern in one's ethnic tradition, expectations of intimacy will probably not be very high.

Although our personal, cultural, and subcultural situations crucially affect the way we approach the journey of intimacy and limit its possibilities, there is a fundamental similarity to each journey. The same insistent call to intimacy, with its stages and phases, promises and perils, comes to all peoples and all classes as part of being human. In this book I hope to focus on the fundamental features of this common human calling to intimacy with its typical patterns and various stages. I do so in the full realization that my descriptions come out of my background and experience and are shaped in terms of my socialization as a middle-class Christian male in North America in the late twentieth century. I invite all my readers from different backgrounds and experiences to join the discussion, to use what is helpful for them, and to make the necessary adjustments to their own situations. In this way we can learn from each other and encourage each other in our common search for intimate relations that satisfy the yearnings of the human spirit.

The five stages are only a general map for marriage. Couples and marriages vary. Each marriage will develop its own particular rhythm and style of movement. Not every marriage will experience each stage with the same intensity or at the same chronological time, and the different stages will mean different things to different couples. Since each of the partners is a unique person and has his or her personal "step-style," as Gail Sheehy calls it, even the partners in a marriage will often experience the stages in markedly different ways. And, we must not forget that every marriage bears the indelible stamp of the culture and subculture in which it exists. But despite the diversity of marriages, both in cultural and individual terms, each journey of intimacy shares common features, phases, and stages. Even though we set sail in our own craft, all of us are sailing on the same Seas of Marriage. Every committed relationship must negotiate a certain sequence of passages if it is to become the deeply fulfilling gift that God intends for us.

Perhaps it is well to note that these stages apply to any committed relationship whether or not it is officially certified as a marriage. Indeed, today some couples are moving into Stage Three before they officially marry. People who are involved in a second marriage or relationship also go through the same stage sequence. However, if they have learned from the first experience, their progress through Stage Two can be more of an adjustment than a power struggle. At the same time, special adjustments are often part of a second marriage, especially in relation to children and in the forming of "blended families." I believe that the same stage development is applicable to homosexual relationships and adult friendships. It is hoped that this book will also encourage the deepening of these intimacies.

There is one other important caution. I do not intend to suggest that the movement from stage to stage is simple linear progression. In fact, it seems clear to me that movement from stage to stage is most appropriately described as an advancing spiral. Finding ourselves unable to advance, we circle back to try to get at the root of the problem. Uncovering an old wound, we may experience a dissolving or resolving of the hurt, which opens up a new way to go. Circling back often brings a measure of healing, slowly empowering us to break through the present impasse. So it goes, and none of it is easy. Intimacy is, indeed, a perilous passage, but it is no more perilous and no less rewarding than being human—accepting the gifts and the risks of identity and intimacy.

NEW OPPORTUNITIES

The obstacles to intimacy that surround us and that we discover in ourselves are discouraging features of modern life. However, since defining the problem is half the solution, bringing the obstacles into focus can, in fact, deliver us from a feeling of hopelessness and inevitability. When we know the situation, we know what needs to change, we know where we need help. A path to intimacy can be cleared in spite of the obstacles.

We can work to change our circumstances rather than to be victimized by them. We do not need to settle for whatever happens in our relationship (as if we are merely pawns), nor do we need to be burdened by the illusion of a perfect relationship (as if that were ever possible). Today there are new freedoms for forming and nourishing a mutually satisfying partnership based on the realistic expectations of two equal persons. We are beginning to realize that the myth of marriage as domestic grind and the myth of marriage as domestic bliss have kept us imprisoned too long. We are entering a new era in which women are no longer to be treated as second-class humans, but, in accordance with God's original design for humankind, men and woman will be equal partners. A remarkable legacy of the women's movement is increased opportunity for genuine intimacy between two people who regard themselves as full equals. Intimacy as the mutual, free, and open sharing of inner lives as equal partners is in our day more than ever before an open invitation to be accepted and enjoyed.

That does not mean that the path to intimacy is clear and easy. Given the cultural situation we have described, the dominant values of our technocratic, consumer society, and the roles for which we were socialized in our family of origin, the path to intimacy will still be scary and risky. Ingrained habits are slow to relinquish their hold; old ways die hard. New habits are hard to learn; alternative ways take shape slowly. Nevertheless, if we have a willingness to change, an openness to learning, a commitment to each other, and the availability of support, we have the opportunity for achieving deeper levels of intimacy for couples on a wider scale than ever before.

2. Identity and Intimacy

The greatest danger, that of losing one's self, may pass off quietly as if it were nothing; every other loss, that of an arm, a leg, five dollars, etc., is sure to be noticed.

— SØREN KIERKEGAARD

The fundamental fact of human existence is [hu]man with [hu]man . . . . All actual life is encounter.

— MARTIN BUBER

The best preparation for intimacy, paradoxical as it may seem, is the establishment and growth of each of us as a separate self. Unless we have a clear sense of self-identity, we do not possess the presence to self to be present to another person. Lacking a bounded sense of self, we reach out for intimacy, not in the first place to give and share ourselves, but to find a base and boundary for our own identity. Before we can freely give ourselves to the intimacies of love, we need to be secure in our own self-identity. The more tenuous our sense of self-identity, the more frightened we are to reach out to other people; inside we retreat from intimacy. But at the same time, our inner need drives us to establish an identity base somewhere, often in a premature marriage or in the confining ideology of a cause.

Self-identity prepares us for intimacy, and intimacy generates a stronger sense of self-identity. The mutually supportive interaction between identity and intimacy is the woof and warp of the fabric of human life. Both our being an individual self and being a member of humankind are gifts of God. Humanity is cohumanity; every I is the "I" of "We." The gifts are simultaneously calls; *Gabe* is *Aufgabe*. The gift of identity is the call to self-identity. The gift of neighbors is the call to intimacy. We are called to accept and develop our gifts of identity and intimacy in partnership with each other, in care for the creation, and in copartnership with with the Giver/Caller. That is the fundamental message of Jesus: love the Lord your God with all your heart, with all your soul, and with all your mind. And love your neighbor as yourself (Matt. 22:37–39).

THE PROBLEM OF SELF-IDENTITY

Love of God and neighbor, says Jesus, is inextricably and reciprocally related to love of self. Genuine intimacy requires self-identity (intimacy with self), just as self-identity requires intimacy with others and intimacy with God (faith). If we lack a sense of self, we have no basis for intimacy, since the communion of love requires two separate identities. Our attempts to establish identity through marriage are, therefore, hazardous in the extreme.

Usually we make the problem worse because we don't really know what we are doing. Presumably we are choosing a marriage partner to fulfill our intimacy needs. What we don't know is that at bottom we are serving our deepest identity needs. Instead of negotiating the rocky passage to self-identity on our own, we are looking to marriage for a solution. Our society too feeds the illusion that joining our fortune with that of another person in marriage is an excellent way to resolve the quest for self-identity. But just as having children does not resolve a marital crisis, neither does marrying resolve the identity question. In fact, by seeking our identity in marriage, we dramatically lower the odds for achieving the very intimacy and fulfillment we desire.

When our identity is so wrapped up in our marriage that our existence is defined in terms of being a husband or wife, our total happiness as a person depends on our marriage. The pressure mounts as each of the partners begins to experience the union as a collusion of needs rather than a sharing of selves. All the eggs are in the marital basket. If they break, the partners will be totally broken as persons. The pressure to come through for each other acts to stifle the spontaneity and freedom crucial to growth in intimacy. Such a marriage may provide security, but at the high cost of claiming all of our time, all of our energy, all of ourselves. It is like the security of a prison; we are safe, but not free. Under constant stress to deliver happiness, such a marriage either stagnates, slowly unravels, or suddenly collapses. If that is marriage, no wonder many people are reacting against it in the name of personal freedom and they have a point.

The problem of attaining and maintaining self-identity in our culture is particularly difficult because of the stereotypes to which we have been socialized as children. As we noted in the previous chapter, women grow up learning that their identity is achieved through connectedness. As a result, many women simply do not distinguish between their identity needs and their intimacy needs. It was in a workshop over ten years ago that this fact really became clear to me. Almost without exception the women introduced themselves as someone's wife or mother. I can still see the totally blank look on their faces when I responded. "Okay, being wives and mothers is very important for you, but those are roles that you fulfill. I was asking, 'Who are you?'" At the end of the day, a thirty-eight-year-old woman hesitantly shared that she had never really faced that question before and, now that she did, she was extremely upset because she could only answer, "I don't know!" I have come to realize that this was not an isolated incident. Until very recent history, a "self-identity" as distinct from an intimacy role was not a genuine possibility for many women in North America.

At the same time, men are also victims of our socialization practices. Learning that their identity is in their separateness, they are wary of intimacy and defend themselves well against it. Men grow up learning that it is wrong to let down, to be weak, dependent, and vulnerable. They deny or try to deny those parts of themselves and try to put up a front of self-sufficiency, control, and confidence. At the same time, as especially Luise Eichenbaum and Susie Orbach have noted, growing up with the confidence that their deepest needs will be taken care of by women, they seek marriage.[1]

But when women enter marriage seeking identity through connection and men enter marriage seeking solace without having to give up their separateness, both men and women suffer. Since men tend to be wary of intimacy, women often do not experience the deep connection they need for their own identity in marriage. Often this leads women to see mothering as the way to experience the connection that will provide a sense of self. However, this too becomes a catch-22 since the mother-infant connection fosters the blurring more than the forming of self-boundaries. Since women tend to find their identity in their intimate relations, men often subconsciously feel pressured and hold back for fear of engulfment.

Women in our culture have often been victimized the most by the practice of seeking identity in marriage. And when this is their self-perception, they naturally "nag" their husbands to give all of themselves to the marriage as well. Henpecked husbands such as Dagwood Bumstead and Fred Flintstone have become fixtures on the cultural scene. Indeed, as many commentators have noted, the romantic myth about marriage is balanced by the cynical myth about marriage as a domestic grind. Happy marriages, it is said, do not exist. For women marriage is a "trap" with four walls and a husband as a keeper. For men marriage is a "trap" set by women. "Marriage," as I read in a novel recently, "is not a word; it's a sentence."

For many, if not most, of us the first and major problem of marriage is a crisis of self-identity. In the first blush of love, the problems are largely invisible (at least we are blind to them). Only later, when our self-identity needs resurface, do we begin to sense the massive dimensions of the problem. We have become so entangled in each other's needs that the marriage threatens our emerging selves. Marriage, to purloin David Cooper's description of the family, has become a "fur-lined bear trap."

FRANK AND ANDREA

Andrea came to therapy because she was in inner turmoil. But since she had a nice home, two children, a nursing career, and a husband who was a good provider, a thoughtful father, and an excellent handyman around the house, she was burdened with guilt. What more could she want? At the same time, she did not feel in inner contact with Frank: "He never talks. I don't know where he is. He's always watching TV and then I feel invisible." She would hold her frustration in so long and then blurt out her complaints to him, browbeat him, and throw a tantrum. When pushed into a corner, he would finally yell back. Feeling like a bad little girl who had crossed Daddy, she would then take it all back, crying, "I'm never good enough. I never do it right." Feeling like a scared little boy who had dared to say no to Momma, he would assure her that he would try harder to meet her needs. For a while he sought refuge in the bed of another woman who didn't "constantly hammer him," who didn't always "want, want, want." Once in the middle of the night, Andrea literally pulled him out of the other bed and brought him home.

Andrea had tried to find her identity in the marriage. She had never felt connected with her mother. She had felt contact with her father but he had committed suicide, and that was just after the "betrayal" of selling the red car he had given her on her birthday. Shortly after her father's death, she had met Frank, felt sorry for him, and felt that she could make him happy. At the same time, lacking a sense of her own self, she looked to Frank for life and love. If Frank was silent, she felt rejected, used, and "invisible." Only when she got through to him did she feel secure. Frank married Andrea because he felt that she was a strong woman who could meet his needs, but he soon felt under constant pressure. Just like his mother, Andrea always wanted more and more, and he felt completely unable to satisfy the never ending "wants." He clammed up. She felt discounted but afraid to speak out for fear that he would leave. But then her needs would get the best of her: "Then, I become a witch." Frank felt bewildered and tried his best to avoid crossing her, growing more defeated and resentful by the day. Finally, he left. At first she felt a sense of freedom when he left, free from being on call to meet his needs. But underneath she felt a panic and heard an inner voice, "I want Daddy."

In therapy Andrea and Frank are beginning to be able to read each other's underlying messages rather than the superficial "She's trying to get" and "He's shutting me out." Andrea is learning that Frank is not constantly rejecting her. He is saying, "Accept me as I am. Give me some space." She is learning that her constant hammering stems from her low self-image. She is growing in understanding that Frank does not need to be forced to say that he cares. He will, in his time and in his own way, express his love freely. Frank is learning that Andrea is not constantly putting him down. She is saying: "I need to hear that you love me. Please tell me." He is learning that his continual retreat has to do with his own deep feelings of inadequacy. As he learns to stand up to her, Andrea is beginning to learn that Frank cannot be her source of life. He is learning to dismantle his defenses and share of his inner self. Both of them are slowly developing a sense of their own boundaries.

A ROBUST SENSE OF SELF

Avoiding marriage (or any kind of intimacy) is an alternative attractive to many today. But the alternative of avoidance is also a sentence, a sentence to loneliness and isolation. Moreover, as we noted above, the experience of intimacy is as integral to self-identity formation as self-identity is to intimacy formation.

Another, far better alternative is to be better prepared for marriage and that means developing a robust sense of self. Nurturing a robust sense of self is of course a lifelong project. Our personhood is not a once-and-for-all, ready-made given. Human life is a dynamic, ongoing process of identity-in-intimacy which is lived out in its stages from conception to death and beyond death. What and who we are is filled out—fulfilled—as life moves on.

Growth is never completed. We can never say that we have arrived. We are always called to new growth and new integrations of self. Such redefinitions of self as we move through the seasons of our life's journey are necessary and crucial if we are to remain living and facing the new challenges that belong to each new stage of life.

However, all the developments and reintegrations are developments and reintegrations of the self as a permanent, personal reality. As a self in the process of growth and change, we remain a personal being with a continuity of identity. This inner self—what the Scriptures refer to as the heart—is the center of reference, identity, and action through all change and development. If this continuity falls away, as it does in schizophrenia, we lose contact with reality. Not having a sense of personal history, of self-sameness through the passage of time, is at the heart of psychosis.

Personal identity, that elusive but continuous individual uniqueness as the self we are, is a given of our humanness, a gift from the Giver of Life. Realizing and appropriating that identity, questing, making it our own, and filling it out is the call of our humanness, a call from the Creator. Self-identity, as

gift and call, develops in relation to other persons who are themselves to us both the gifts and calls of intimacy.

IDENTITY AND ROOTS

As a unique person, I am an identity in my own right from
the beginning of my life. In the course of my life I become
richer, deeper, and more secure in myself as I ground, sense,
and integrate my identity. Without grounding I am "in the air,"
unsure of my footing, uprooted, and ultimately lost in the universe.[2] Without a sense of self I remain out of touch with myself,
inert and passive. Without an integrated sense of self, I am fragmented and internally at odds with myself. My sense of self-
identity is enhanced when I experience myself as an active agent,
a center of intention, an intentional doer working for harmony
and unity among the fragmented and unbalanced sides of my
life.

Indispensable to healthy self-identity is grounding. To be
grounded is to experience within myself secure connection to
the basic realities of my existence. It is to know bodily that the
earth is a place I can safely put my feet down on. I identify with
my body, accept my sexuality, and have roots that sustain and
nourish me. I know where I stand; I feel my space. My connection within myself to other persons, to all the creatures of
creation, and ultimately with God gives me reason to be in the
world. My connection with God is the primal ground of my existence. Rooted in creation and the God of creation, I am at
home, I belong, I count, I make a difference—despite evil and
suffering. I know that the ground of life is not far away or hostile. God is my certain ground.

In faith I experience my reality as gifted, graced, and
grounded. I know who I am: a male or female agent of God's
love, caretaker of creation, and a member of the human community. I know where I am: in the complex, intricate, often
alienating but good creation of God which was made to be our
home. I know what I need: reconnection with self, others, the
universe, and God. I know where I am headed: a renewed creation where peace and justice shall reign in spite of sin and evil.
In the ultimate commitment of faith, grounded in God, I ap-

propriate to myself a personal framework to make sense of reality and to integrate my experience.

AN INTEGRATED SENSE OF IDENTITY

But a healthy self-identity requires more than entrustment to God and a personal vision of life's meaning. We need a sense of ourselves, vigorous and open, sensitive and flowing, in touch with the full range of human emotions. One of the worst things that can happen to any of us is to have no sense of self and to be so absent from ourselves that we are no longer conscious of our situation. It's much better to feel our unhappiness, for then at least we feel alive. Feeling our joy, sorrow, anger, anxiety, and despair places us in vibrant touch with ourselves and life around us. We are motivated to action. Being in touch with our deepest fears and hopes, aware of our built-in defenses, we develop an opened sense of self that acknowledges both our virtues and our limitations. We learn a deeper sense of self-acceptance that cuts through any debasement or aggrandizement of self.

Healthy self-knowledge comes not only from being in touch with ourselves and our processes, but from a growing ability to know when we are out of touch. We know when we are safely ensconced in our battlements, unwilling or unable to come out. We know the difference between being well defended and being vulnerable. We sense when we are giving and when we are demanding, when we are taking rather than asking. We see ourselves consistently neither as the greatest of God's gifts to the world nor as the least of all creatures. Growing self-acceptance comes through giving up rationalizing, projecting, blaming, and excusing. Instead of denying it, I own my part; instead of blaming myself, I accept the adventure of being who I am. Giving up my illusions of control, I accept my be-ing. I come to know myself in deeper and deeper ways, with a sense of self rooted in my internal being rather than in my external doing.

Growing in self-identity is gaining a centered sense of my identity in which I do not deny or repress sides of myself. I grow in owning all of myself, including the weak and fearful, the powerful and vulnerable. Men fully own their intuitive, emotional side. Women get in touch with their assertive, independent self.

All of us work for an increased sense of our unity and integration of the many sides of our existence. Through the painful process of learning limits and strengths, we integrate into our self-image what we can and what we cannot do. We work to make our personality work for us rather than against us. With a strong sense of self and with an awareness of our gifts, we have the motivation and personal integration to live out and enjoy what we accept to be the meaning and purpose of our life.

IDENTITY AND INTIMACY

With a centered sense of self comes a bounded sense of self: I know my boundaries. This is crucial, for without a sense of my space, reaching out and relating to others is filled with deep and primal anxieties. I want to be close, but I'm afraid to be close. I fear engulfment by another and loss of self, or I fear invasion because my boundaries are so fragile. I'm divided: I want intrusion because I feel empty, but I fear intrusion because it threatens my fragile self.

In our culture, as we have mentioned, men generally appear to have more difficulty with connection and females more difficulty with separateness. Men are socialized to keep their separate identity well defended; women are socialized to be connected to others in the world. Consequently when man and woman deeply connect "the response is patterned and predictable. He fears engulfment; she fears invasion."[3] Both fear intimacy. Wanting to defend against their dependency needs, men tend to withdraw into their separate selves. Intimacy brings out repressed needs and the fear of engulfment. Desirous of making deep attachments, women do not develop their separate boundaries as fully and firmly as males. Intimacy activates the fear that the boundaries of self are too permeable.

Although Lillian Rubin's main point about men and women seems well taken, my own therapeutic experience and study suggest that she goes too far when she follows Nancy Chodorow in believing that "*the basic* feminine sense of self is connected to [others in] the world," and "*the basic* masculine sense of self is separate."[4] Not-good-enough mothering in the first months of life may leave women as well as men without any sense of connectedness. Similarly, not-good-enough mothering may leave men as well as women without any sense of separateness. Such people, male and female, have little or no sense of their own boundaries. They have what is often called a "borderline personality." Having no developed inner sense of self as either connected or separate, their sense of identity is without borders, scattered and unintegrated. Such people seek fusion with another person to give themselves borders. Sometimes they may be like revolving doors, completely "occupied" by whomever they are with for the moment. Sometimes their borderline, extremely fluid sense of self leads them into marriages in which they are deeply fused with their partners. In a moment we will look more carefully at the "enmeshed marriages" which result from both partners having a borderline personality.

My point here is that on this fundamental level maleness or femaleness is of no account. At least it seems very problematic to maintain that every woman by nature has a sense of connection and every man by nature a sense of separation. At the same time, I do agree that in general in our society men are socialized to present more of a separate self to the world as part of the male role and that women are generally socialized to develop less self-contained and more reaching-out personalities. But this is a difference, I suspect, on the level of the "presenting" or "social self" and not a difference of "inner" or "core" self. The social self of most men in our society is more separate and the social self of most women is more connected. But, as many of us know, our social self may be quite different than our inner self. Men may develop a separate social self as a defensive cover against lack of any boundaries. Women may develop a connected social self as a defensive cover against lack of any deep internal connection with anyone else.

Whatever the impact of being male and female, it is certainly true that identity and intimacy go hand in hand for both sexes. When we have a good sense about ourselves and know our boundaries, we need not fear connection with another. Indeed, we will reach out with open hearts for intimacy. When we are present to self, grounded in our space, flowing, connected with our inner self, we can be present with another without needing to use him or her for our own benefit. Self-availability and availability to another are mutually interdependent. As I begin to enjoy being me, I can more easily take joy in the mystery of the other.

If we have a poorly integrated sense of self or virtually lack a sense of self, we are only vaguely present to ourselves. We are not able to experience ourselves consistently throughout time as a person with a past moving toward a future. We tend also to be amnesiac. Not flowing or present to ourselves, it is hard to really be present in our doing. Often we feel disconnected with what we are doing and force ourselves to go through the motions even as we feel lost and bored to death with our existence. Sometimes we lose ourselves in a regimented treadmill existence, which we dare not give up lest we unleash the inner panic of not feeling connected. Experiencing inner emptiness, we struggle with contradictory self-perceptions and consequently, to our utter dismay, we engage in contradictory actions.

Being at ease with others is virtually impossible for one who is in dis-ease with self. We may see others the way we see ourselves: flat, empty, and impoverished or chaotic, seething, and scattered. We may fear to let other people into our lives because we project on them our own unfulfilled yearnings. Our basic posture is aloneness. We may also may have idealized and fantasized perceptions of others that match our fantasies about ourselves.

If such is our relation to ourselves, our relations to others will most likely be chaotic, shallow, and nonempathetic. Our intimacies will often turn out to be collusions. We become blindly entangled in each other's needs and fantasies. Our relations to others are often basically salvage efforts to shore up our fragile selves. Rather than the rich intimacy of partners we hope for, we often end up in a safe dovetailing with someone who remains a stranger because we are both estranged from ourselves.

When we lack a bounded sense of self, we do not have a sense of our constancy. Feeling disconnected and insecure, we yearn for union with another to give us definition and boundaries. Marriage is a way to satisfy that longing. However, since we need a sense of self-boundaries and self-constancy before we can have a sense of the partner's constancy, separation from our loved one becomes difficult to tolerate. Since we lack a constant, internalized representation of our partner, during his or her absense we have no sense of his or her reality. We feel at loose ends, as if we have lost contact with ourselves. We lack boundaries and self-definition. At the same time, extreme dependence on a loved one becomes difficult to tolerate. Differences of any kind confuse: we are one; why do we disagree? Can we disagree? We can be so dependent on the other person that we may begin to hate him or her for meaning too much to us. We can't live alone, but neither can we live together. Finding our boundaries in each other, we are as deeply dependent on our partner as we are deeply resentful about that bondage. In such borderline situations terms of endearment, as in the movie, become terms of enmeshment.

Although it is true that we often remain strangers to each other, blocks of stone, hard and cold, unable to melt and flow, that is not the way we were made. God meant for our souls to touch and commune, to dance and play together in the exquisite rituals of human intimacy. To be a full person is to be in full communion. To relate is central to what it means to be human. Each "I" is an "I" of the "We" of humanity. And the "We" is indissolubly bound up with all the family of creation and with God.

We begin our lives in another person. The meaning of our birth is separation from mother, for one soul cannot remain in another. Growing up to self-identity is a matter of separating from parents, individuating, finding our own ground and boundedness. But this sense of personal self develops from the beginning in interaction with other selves. And when finally we come to know our centeredness, having settled in and come to terms with self, we are ready to move outward with a minimum of fear and desperation, ready to begin to form a new unity that can over time give rise to other persons.

Identity-in-intimacy, intimacy-with-identity is the rhythm of the dance of life. Identity as presence-to-and-with-self develops in interaction with intimacy as presence-to-and-with-another. Identity is as fundamental to intimacy as intimacy is to identity.[5] Each is required to experience the other. In the beginning I see myself in mother's eyes. Along with my mother's milk, I drink in a fledging sense of self. Learning to trust her, I learn to trust myself. Without her, I am lost to myself. Finding her again, I find myself. How well each of us negotiates the delicate four-stage process of separating and individuating in the first three years of life (described so well by Margaret Mahler and associates) says much about how we will negotiate our adult experiences of identity and intimacy.[6]

Discovering my sense of self-worth in being received, I venture out to discover my unique identity. I need the affirmation of intimacy to move out in self-affirmation. And at the same time, I need an affirmative sense of my own identity to risk intimacy with another. The two movements belong together. The better we get to know ourselves, the closer we can get to each other. A strong sense of identity is realized in and through a deep intimacy with others. A deep sense of intimacy develops in people who have a strong sense of themselves. Connecting with others feeds our own sense of well-being. Missed connections can lead us to close us down in despair.

In true intimacy we surrender ourselves to each other freely, and both of us are enhanced, enriched, and feel more ourselves. It is a relation rich in paradox and promise. Reaching out from myself, risking self, meeting another self, surrendering self, I enlarge my sense of self. The dance continues. We begin to risk deeper and deeper levels of self and intimacy flourishes.

FALSE OPTIONS: AUTONOMY AND SUBMISSION

It is important to give attention to the dance of interdependence between identity and intimacy, especially today when so many of us experience our intimate union as a trap in which we lose our identity. Our calling from God is to work out identity-in-intimacy without isolating ourselves in false autonomy or debasing ourselves in false submission to another.

Both false options are driven by the basic dynamics of sin. We have long recognized the dark side of autonomy and self-inflation, but not always of submission and self-deflation. Deflation and underesteem of self are as wrong as overinflation and pride.

Actually, to find self-esteem through submission to another person is in the end a subtle way to self-inflation: I share in the honor and glory of the person to whom I submit. Figure 1 diagrams the identity-intimacy interaction and the false options of autonomy and submission.

Let me say this more simply. For many of us sin is being selfish and thinking too much of self. We think and act as if the biblical way is to be selfless. Indeed, traditional socialization patterns in the West have encouraged passivity, masochism, and self-disparagement particularly in women. But isn't that every bit as dehumanizing as self-aggrandizement, and as sinful?

Actually, both inflation and deflation of self result not from thinking too much but too little of self. A posture of pride and self-sufficiency covers over the nagging fear that our inner self is too weak to withstand the vulnerability of intimacy. Or if we are stricken by feelings of inadequacy and inferiority, we over-invest in another in order to satiate our empty souls and achieve total security.

Both over- and underinflation of self are defensive maneuvers covering a fundamental lack of accepting ourselves as gifted-but-limited.[7] On the one hand, fantasizing ourselves to be gods, we consider ourselves to be all-sufficient and without limitations. On the other hand, fearing that we are nonentities, we deny our creative gifts and resign ourselves to powerlessness. We dominate another to play out our fantasy of being a god or we are dominated by another to play out our illusion that we are totally helpless and useless. Often, in fact, the two illusions feed on each other. We fantasize that we are gods to cover up the secret fear of death, impotence, and ignominy. We allow ourselves to be dominated to cover up the secret belief that we are superior.

Each of us can employ a variety of guises to hide from God, others, and ourselves the basic dis-ease at the heart of our being: separation from God, from self, from other persons, and from creation. Lacking the connection with self, others, and creation that comes from surrendering ourselves to God and God's way of love and justice, we pretend to be a god or become slavishly dependent on others to fabricate a sense of certainty and identity. In our supposed superiority we do violence to others, or in

E
X   Deflation of self
T   Submission to others
R   Abandonment: "I can't live without you"
E   Fear of emptiness: Advance
M   Overinvestment
E

Present-with-others

WE Intimacy

G
O ← Faith —— **LOVE** —— Care → **CREATION**
D

I Identity

Present-to-self
Independent
Single

E
X   Underinvestment
T   Fear of Invasion: Retreat
R   Inner isolation: "I don't need anyone"
E   Domination of others
M   Inflation of self: Autonomy
E

Figure One

our assumed inferiority we turn the violence on ourselves. We defy God by playing god or by an abdication of our responsibility. We try to save ourselves or we point the finger at someone else.

LETTING GO AND FINDING SELF

Jesus had these self-serving dynamics in mind when he warned that "anyone who tries to preserve his life will lose it, and anyone who loses it will keep it safe" (Luke 17:33). The "losing" of self that Jesus describes is not the false humility of self-debasement. It is the letting go of the narcissistic will to control or be controlled. It is the finding of self through surrender ("losing") to the God who made and saves us. Rooting our identity in intimacy with God, we are renewed to wholeness and empowered in the Spirit to lives of freedom and intimacy with self, others, and all of creation.

This "losing" of self is in no way a losing of self-esteem or self-love. From the humility of surrender to God flows legitimate love of self, self-acceptance, and self-renewal. Such love of self, rooted in loving intimacy with God, is of one piece with love of others. Such are the identity-intimacy dynamics we have been exploring. Since I am human and you are human, to love others is to love myself as well as you. In giving myself to you in the intimacy of love, I am fulfilling myself.

In all of this I can only conclude that selfishness and lack of genuine intimacy are not caused by too much identity, so to speak, but by too little. Actually, it is not less sense of self that is needed for intimacy, but more. When I grow in my sense of self, I am able to give you more space. I don't need to pull on you neurotically for acceptance and affirmation or pull back from you, fearing engulfment, when you reach out in need. In my growing strength, I can take you in as the person you are rather than as the person I want you to be.

With a healthy sense of my gifts and limits, I do not need to demand that you make me happy, nor am I obliged to make you come alive. I can let you be because I am learning to let myself be. And such letting be is what love is all about. Then I am ready to reach out to you with open heart. I need not run from intimacy, nor need I demand entrance. I do not need to live in isolation or in servile dependency. Secure in our identity we are free to be intimate. We can meet in the middle. Identity is not self-serving autonomy, nor is intimacy self-deprecating submission. Meeting in the middle breaks the vicious circle of the "powerful" and the "powerless" that has trapped us for too long. Persons in their own right, males and females are empowered to be vulnerable in intimacy.

This intimacy-with-identity model shows the folly of extremist programs that encourage women to emulate the "masculine" model and put Number One first. Instead of being gracious givers, it is said, women have to become hard-nosed takers. But in this way the exile of intimacy continues: giving is the very electricity of intimacy. For the sake of all of us, women need to continue to give and care. They also need to insist that men give and care in return. Men need to own their tender and gentle side and women need to own their own assertive and strong side. For it is only in the mutual giving and receiving of two equals that true partnership exists—and true love.

ADOLESCENCE: THE SEARCH FOR SELF-IDENTITY

We are who we are. And we become who we are. Becoming the person I am is a development that commences with my beginning, carries over into infancy, adolescence, adulthood, old age, death, and beyond. Each new stage of life brings with it new challenges and opportunities. When we fail to respond adequately to the new challenges, we diminish or fragment our identity; we close down our humanity and become less than we are called to be.

It is during adolescence that the calling to know oneself as a person becomes particularly insistent. Prior to adolescence, we are, of course, an individual identity who begins to take shape at the moment of conception and continues in interaction with other persons and the environment. Indeed the fundamentals of our personality structure are already formed by age six. But before adolescence, the sense of being a separate, unique person with our own identity, male or female, is not so much struggled with as assumed.

With the beginning of adolescence, however, the question of self-identity becomes the overriding and pivotal concern. There is a self-conscious focus on being a separate person, separate from mother and father, separate from friends, a unique free-standing man or woman. That's why Erik Erikson calls the question of self-identity the developmental calling of the adolescent stage, a calling that requires positive resolution before a person is prepared to face the challenge of "intimacy" typical of early adulthood. How am I different from and yet related to significant others? Only when I know, accept, and trust myself, can I come of age as a maturing adult ready for a life partner and a life project.

Adolescence has been called a "second individuation," which follows on the first separation-individuation process that takes place between six months and thirty months, and so it is. Living through rapid and multiple changes within and without, I am a physical, emotional, cognitive, social, political, moral, and religious being, and in all these ways I face the question of self.[8] I set out in quest of self-identity. Trying to find self, I am afraid to lose self. Trying to make a difference, I am sure that I make no difference. Wanting to leave home, I don't want to leave home. The fear of being an adult pushes me backward to being a child; the fear of remaining a child propels me forward to taking adult responsibility. I feel so vulnerable and awkward. The high rate of adolescent suicide and adolescent pregnancy bear eloquent witness to the difficulties in dealing with these conflicting feelings and pressures.

In these challenging years between childhood and adulthood, I achieve (or fail to achieve) a self-conscious sense of my center, and I appropriate (or fail to appropriate) a unifying and anchoring purpose for my life as a whole. This burgeoning and blossoming of self as center of reference, intention, and action takes shape gradually through the challenges I face in integrating the totality of my past experience and in making new choices for my future development. Self-identity grows as I learn to take myself seriously as a person who can choose, a person who is active and powerful on my own behalf. Self-identity is not so much a given that can be described as a place where I am at home with self. It is not so much that my identity is set and I know what I will do; rather, I experience a growing familiarity with my own space, its limits and its strengths. I have a home base from which to reach out, change, grow, and be open.

It is this persisting identity, grounded and self-aware, that provides the basis for lasting relationships with others. It is this self that is held responsible, the inner core to which others appeal and on which they rely. Without a persistent sense of self, lasting commitments are as ill-advised as they are impossible.

In a society that itself is in turmoil, adolescents are subject to intense pressures. It becomes even more hazardous to separate from parents if the bond with them was weak or overanxious during early childhood (birth to two years). Without good bonding, separation is difficult. Wanting to but unable to separate, many adolescents search for ways to avoid the dilemma. Overwhelmed by the choice, young men and women easily slide into a false resolution of their identity.

Parents who were unable to develop a "good-enough"[9] bond with their infant children either overinvest or underinvest in them throughout their lives. However, both smothering and abandoning deprive children of the loving support they need to sustain their quest for identity. During adolescence well-intentioned parents often push and peddle their ways on their youth to save them from decision and turmoil. But they are actually abdicating true parental responsibility when they do not provide the room, understanding, and support that allow adolescents to make their own decisions in their own time. The agony, loneliness, and struggle of adolescence needs to be lived through, not detoured, bridged over, or denied. If the journey is not completed in adolescence, sooner or later the journey will have to be renegotiated.

Parental smothering and overinvestment are accompanied, often in the same family, by underinvestment and abandonment, the one parent smothering, the other abandoning. Such over- and under-attention further unsettles and disorients the adolescent. Adolescents need unencumbered space for self-formation and they need support. Without support they gradually turn in on themselves, cold and disheartened—even when they put on a veneer of bravado. Leaving home and finding self emotionally (if not necessarily physically) is the adolescent's task. But adolescents can only truly leave home in strength and with a measure of confidence when they experience the warm support, care, and interest of their parents and parental figures. In the absence of such care, they "run" from home or are "turfed out," feeling abandoned, uncared for, and rebellious—or they may stay put at home, unable to face the world at large.

In a climate of under- and overinvestment, adolescents are unable to separate cleanly and truly from their parents. They make the best of their dilemma by three kinds of basic response patterns. They submit and become "good" (pleasing their parents); they resist, act up, and become "bad" (punishing their parents); or they refuse to grow up (frustrating their parents). Thus, we have pleasers, resisters, and postponers, not unlike Sam Keen's categories of Pleasers, Nice People, and Sentimentalists; Adversaries; and Romantics, Idealists, Playboys, and Playgirls.[10] But these patterns prevent adolescents from developing a solid sense of their own identity. The quest for personal identity is sidetracked into a sometimes conscious but more often unconscious campaign to win parental approval by pleasing, to revenge parental inattention through defiance, or to cover over the confusion and agony by prolonging adolescence and postponing commitment. Pleasing is a way of not really separating. Resisting is a way of trying to force a separation. Postponing is a way of not separating by escaping into a romantic or sexual idealism. It is important to know the dynamics of these patterns so that we do not define adolescents only in terms of these defensive postures. Realizing that these patterns are survival mechanisms formed in frustration and hurt, we are enabled to see beyond them and honor the deeper, underlying struggles for self-expression and self-esteem. Then, we are in position to offer our adolescents genuine support and help.

PLEASING

Pleasing is a common way of dealing with the inability to separate. Pleasers don't make trouble, but neither are they exciting and vibrant. Instead of finding their own center and establishing their own boundaries, adolescents become what parental figures want them to be, hoping to cajole acceptance. But when adjusting and accommodating to the demands of authority becomes a way of acting in the world, it is difficult for a sense of personal power and self-confidence to develop. Pleasers try to smile away the problems of life: they are the "nice" people—at least on the outside. On the inside, they often nourish secret grudges. After all, since they only do what others say they should do, why should they suffer when things go wrong. Others are to blame. The repressed negativity may show itself in ulcers and depression or it may erupt in rage.

Much in our society promotes this solution. Don't ask too many questions. Fall in step. Do what you are told, and you will be well liked, well adjusted, and successful. No wonder so many of us become what our parents or society want us to become: we dress and behave to elicit approval; we even choose mates, careers, and churches that will fulfill parental hopes. But when important personal decisions are made more out of a felt need to please and appease than out of the throes of struggles to know our own gifts and hopes, we can easily be deeply hurt and extremely unhappy. Sometimes, no doubt, we may end up with choices that we do learn to make our own. But just as often, if not more often, we find ourselves saddled with choices that go against our personal grain. An identity is forged in the crucible of decision. If adolescents are spoon-fed solutions, they are deprived of the very struggles out of which their emerging identity takes form.

Sadly, an abiding ethos that good girls and boys cause no problems for their parents or society continues to encourage "easy" decisions. Sadly, as many of us are discovering in a mid-life crisis, there is a high price to pay. One day we wake up realizing that we are not happy and never have been really happy with what has happened to us. We realize that we don't really know ourselves. It is as if the people and career decisions we made were foisted upon us without our heart's full involvement. Once upon a time, provoked by an inability to separate, we let the needs and wishes of others become the weather vane of our identity.

Parents need to be keenly aware of adolescents' deep sensitivity to parental approval and disapproval. The apparent indifference of adolescents toward parents is only an indication of how sensitive they are inside. Sometimes fear of disapproval not only leads them to please for the sake of pleasing, but they hide their need for approval even from themselves. For this reason parents need to go out of their way to provide assurances of love and support even as they encourage adolescents to make their own choices. And if they sense deep insecurity, a longer period of time for the process of leaving home, extended support, and encouragement may be necessary.

RESISTING

Resisting, rather than pleasing, is also a common pattern of dealing with the need for but fear of separating. Resisters find themselves in being negative as a way to emphasize their separation. When we live out of such a negative identity, we feel most alive when we are in opposition. If there is nothing to complain about, we can't rest until there is. Saying no becomes second nature, even if we defeat ourselves as well. In extreme cases, even suicide is a possibility as long as it pays back our parents for not caring. We vent our rage on society for we are the wronged. Or we can become paranoid, denying our rage and projecting it on others. The world is out to get us. Disaster, we fear, follows us around like a shadow.

Resisting for the sake of resisting can become a self-defeating posture for an adolescent. But, we need to remember that saying no before saying yes is an indispensable ingredient of adolescence. Only in that way are young people able to form their own identities and decide that they, rather than their parents, peers, or society, want to embrace this career, worship this God, or marry this person. Strong pressures to force adolescents to decide before they are ready as well as the approval promised to those who please makes support for adolescents in their struggle, doubt, and experimentation exceedingly important. If we do not give our young people their rightful space, we often give them little choice but to resist if they want to retain any sense of their own dignity. When the fear of staying dependent and the tendency to be overwhelmed by parental expectations threatens an already too fragile sense of self, parents need to give even more independence and room than usual. We may even know what is right for them, but if we force it upon them we dishonor their fragile spirits. We need to trust that, in due time, adolescents will discover for themselves what is right for them. It is an illusion to believe that we are really helping by rescuing them at every turn. But because we cannot make sure that their lives will be happy, that does not mean that we abandon them. We need to stand with them, assuring them of our support, offering advice rather than dictating solutions, honoring and respecting them as persons in all their struggles and decisions.

Teenagers tell me that they are attracted to "heavy metal" because in the music they are able to identify with and live out feelings of rebellion and frustration they have no other way to express. In fact, it is just the premium on being nice and pretending (even when family life is falling apart and we all live under the nuclear threat) that induces many young people to stay clenched in rebellion. With no support in their struggle, especially if they have also suffered neglect or abuse from their parents, these young people see no choice but to become resisters to defend their fragile sense of self. Some, of course, learn eventually to play the societal game and put on a pleasing front that masks a lasting inner defiance.

POSTPONING

Postponing is also a common option in dealing with the need to separate and individuate. Postponers live in fantasy, pretending they can remain eternally young and carefree, creating an illusion of separation in a romantic, idealized world. They try not to face the issue of self-identity. Trying to live on the surface, losing themselves in externals and immediacies, they avoid making the choices and commitments that give form and substance to personal identity. Faced with all the pressures, they try to stay in control and avoid further hurt by keeping people at a distance. Postponers try to avoid the intensity of the search for identity by removing themselves internally from the fray. They numb themselves to avoid the pain. Perhaps, like water, they can adapt to every container, be at home everywhere. Postponers need help in understanding that postponing is, in fact, a decision to remain uncommitted, for to be at home everywhere is to be home nowhere. Postponing is a way for adolescents to survive when the pressures feel too overwhelming. However, when we look more closely at a postponer, we will often also find pleasing or resisting. Indeed, sometimes when we look more carefully at pleasers and resisters, we will find postponers underneath. Postponing is an intensely lonely posture—and life moves on, reality needs to be faced, and decisions made. To feel a connection and to exercise a degree of power, a postponer will often decide by pleasing or resisting a parent.

Now certainly it is true that adolescents need all the room we can give them in the agony of their struggle. They need time to resolve and consolidate their identity. We should not push them to hurry their process, because too often that means pushing them into becoming pleasers or resisters. Postponement is a valuable period of adolescence when it is part of the painful and lonely struggle of trying out various options. It takes time to come to know ourselves. Again the best parental policy is support that honors adolescent space and timing. When that support is present, adolescents will in their own time take positive steps toward personal identity. Postponers especially need time to bring their romantic ideals down to earth and to test them in reality one by one.

Deep involvement with another person while living in any of these typical patterns is virtually a recipe for disaster, yet the truth is that nearly all of us have adopted one of these patterns to survive. Unconsciously we choose a partner, not first of all for sharing of self, but to compensate for unmet needs. Pleasers look for someone they can control through pleasing and can blame for their unhappiness. They want someone to attach to and avoid separation. Resisters look for someone who can feed their rage and give them a reason for their negativity. They defend their threatened selves by seeking someone they have good reasons to resist. Deeply afraid of facing and testing life with their own resources, postponers look for someone who will collude with them in prolonging the dreams of preadolescence.

"I AM MY BODY"

Pleasing, resisting, and postponing are three broad ways to foreclose the quest for personal identity prematurely. All of them are ways to cope, but they also fragment, or in Erikson's term, "diffuse," our personal identity into various roles. Each of the three patterns may show itself in a wide variety of forms. Often young people turn to their sexuality for their identity, discovering that the power and allure of sex is the best way for them to manipulate approval, vent rage, lose themselves in sensation, find soothing, or continue dependency. The macho male and the *femme fatale* are perhaps the most obvious examples.

However, "I am my body" is really no solution, because such an identity rooted not in self-esteem but in the hormonal response of others is fragile and fleeting. It cannot answer the hidden needs for independence, security, or a sense of power and self. Yet this way is seductive, for it has long been condoned in our society and is the daily fare of advertising and the media. The solution is destructive because locating total personal identity in physical sexuality ignores or denigrates our human needs for inner connection and ultimate meaning, for justice, mercy, and love. The solution fails because the human gift of sexuality becomes an instrument for continuing dependency or forcing separation without the compassion and commitment of shared selves. Physical sexuality is one glorious feature of being human. To ignore it or downplay it is to delude ourselves, but it is no less a delusion to let sexuality be the beginning and end of personal identity.

"I AM MY CAUSE"

Other adolescents turn to a cause, so that in the safety and security of numbers and in the ideals of a cause they can avoid standing on their own feet. Pleasers join and become model, if passive, members of the community, basking in the approval they receive for their faithful service and continued dependency. Resisters join causes that allow them to vent their rage against authority, dividing the world neatly into "us" and "them," safeguarding their fragile sense of self. Postponers tend to disavow causes that might implicate them in real life, preferring to lose themselves in idle fancies or utopian dreams that do not confront them with the realities of implementation.

Joining a cause and contributing to society belongs to the matrix of life. But the joining should emerge out of personal conviction that the cause is noble and just, not out of nagging internal emptiness. Often a cause represents an idealized parental image for the adolescent and joining indicates an unfulfilled need to identify with an admired parent. When the ready-made answers of a cause define our identity, we can very easily become the victims of that cause. We go along with whatever happens for fear of disapproval or excommunication. The deep uncertainty many people experience today makes the seductive pull of cults understandable. On the other hand, provided the cause is worthy, integral, and reality-based, identification with an ideal is a growing and healing experience for people with some bounded sense of self.

"MY MIND IS MY BEING"

Many more adolescents avoid facing their separateness by finding a substitute identity in their intellectual prowess. Impressed by their burgeoning ability to think abstractly, they "find" themselves in their intellect. "My mind is my being." But this security is achieved often at the cost of their emotional, spiritual, and sexual lives. Living in their head appeals to adolescents who have been unable to handle bodily sexual feelings or who repress their emotions. At its best, the "intellect" can provide a frame of reference to help locate ourselves and to help make sense out of our experience, but it can also be a powerful instrument by which we can ingratiate ourselves with others, vent our defiance against the world, or hide from ourselves and others our commitment to noncommitment.

"MARRIAGE IS MY LIFE"

One other solution to the identity crisis that many adolescents choose is the central concern of this book—marriage. It is a particularly understandable and tempting solution, for in the midst of their struggle to separate and establish their own identity, adolescents are faced with the next developmental calling—intimacy. Fueled by the emerging sexual energies of puberty, two young people can use each other to avoid being separate, extend dependency, and acquire a substitute identity. But in doing so, the mutual giving and sharing of intimacy are most often replaced by taking and demanding. Pleasers do "please" their mates, but the mates are made to pay if they do not reciprocate. The pleasing is suspect because it is motivated more by a desire to win approval from the other rather than by a genuine impulse of the heart to care. Resisters often marry in the unconscious hope that their partners will offer them the love they missed during childhood. But stuck in defiance, they need to fight with their mates (and even abuse them physically) to feel alive and powerful. Postponers often resist the confines of marriage or deep friendships, sentencing themselves to lives of loneliness or satiating themselves in a series of superficial relationships. But just as often they get married, since it is the convenient thing to do. As we shall see, pleasers often gravitate toward resisters and vice versa. Postponers seem to prefer postponers. But, since postponers are often also either pleasers or resisters, here too the attraction of opposites appears to hold true.

In our society we have evolved intricate mechanisms and rituals for the dovetailing of our needs. In the beginning, the truth is well hidden, but it cannot be hidden forever, as the current state of marital disarray reveals. Pleasing, resisting, and postponing, whether expressed in sexuality, intellect, or causes, are inadequate—if understandable—ways to answer the question of identity. Coping with the challenges and tensions of adolescence by foreclosing the search and finding ourselves in pleasing and resisting others or in postponing is to ask for frustration and unhappiness. To identify ourselves with only one of our ways of being in the world, whether it be sexuality, emotion, or intellect, restricts and fragments the self. If I see my true self only in my keen analytic mind, my physical and emotional needs become less important. If my life is my physical body, my emotional, intellectual, and spiritual lives suffer. Fixating on one mode of my being in an attempt to define my identity, I lose something more valuable: the unity of myself in many dimensions. Similarly, if my existence is my marriage or my friendship or my job, I enslave myself.

RHODA

Rhoda is a vivacious twenty-six-year-old who after three years of therapy is struggling hard to move beyond the little girl fantasies she has lived with most of her life to the scary but real issues of being an adult woman. She puts it well: "I'm exhausted by not being real." Rhoda grew up feeling like a bad girl out of place in her own family. She soon learned that her looks and manner made her attractive to boys and gave her the attention she craved. She became a princess awaiting the kiss that would make her come alive. During the past ten years she has gone through a series of relationships all of which began with her being swept off her feet and all of which ended with her discovering that there was nothing in it for her. She alternated between missing men, wanting to please them, and being angry with them. She enjoyed the sex, but increasingly, like Annie Hall, she found herself watching herself just going through the motions.

Rhoda needed men to give her life and identity. In therapy Rhoda discovered that her deep insecurity led her to be attracted only to needy, sadistic men who were attracted to her. In meeting their needs, she could control them. "Secure men I can't control." At the same time, in exchange she expected that her needs would be met. So each time she allowed herself to be used until she could take it no more. Then, even though filled with guilt, she would break off the relationship. Looking back on these times, she realizes that she was playing with fire: "I almost gave my life away. My spirit is bruised." Now, instead of running and losing herself in fantasy relationships, she is coming to grips with her inner needs and fears and slowly allowing herself to take the time to find her own sense of self. The process of attaining internal identity and internal peace will be gradual and it will not be easy. She suffers from bouts of nausea and fatigue when her insecurity surfaces. She is also bothered at present by a strange, medically inexplicable rash that covers her skin when exposed to the sun. Her body is encouraging her to let out the griefs and fears that she has held in so long. Slowly she is learning not to seek her identity in her need to please and in her sexual attractiveness to men. Through a solid relationship with her therapist with whom she feels bonded, she is beginning to enjoy the freedom and support to truly become herself. And the more she becomes herself, the more she is preparing herself for the intimacies of a genuine partnership of love.

3. Stage One: Romance

Ah, love, let us be true
To one another! for the world, which seems
To lie before us like a land of dreams,
So various, so beautiful, so new,
Hath really neither joy, nor love, nor light,
Nor certitude, no peace, nor help for pain. . . .

—MATTHEW ARNOLD

The loving life is a two-step dance between the intimacy of bonding and the identity of solitude, coming together and going apart, being together and being alone. The fulfillment of the human promise depends on the nurturing and blossoming of our ability to be vulnerable with others and with ourselves: free-to-be-with (without the fear of engulfment) and free-to-be-apart (without the desperation of loneliness). We come to learn who we are in the rough and tumble of our relations with others.

In leaving home in adolescence, we need and want close friends for bouncing ideas around, sharing fears, and alleviating loneliness. Just as in the first months of life mother serves as mirror of ourselves, so in the birth of adolescence we need friends to be mirrors of our souls. At the same time, driven by our budding sexuality, we begin to yearn for a special person with whom we can share ourselves body and soul in the intimacy of marriage. The winds of romance take hold of our souls. We fall in love. And we marry our prince or princess.

SWEET ROMANCE

The initial stage of the marriage journey is falling in love. Most of us don't quite know how it happens; we just know that it happened! Looking at each other makes our pulse race, touching each other takes our breath away, just talking to each other sets our hearts pounding. And when absent from each other, we are still swept away in daydreams and fantasies of each other. No one else matters. Sometimes romance comes like a bolt of lightning; sometimes it creeps up like the dawn of a glorious summer day. But in any case we are embraced by something that is bigger than both of us; we are happy victims of the malady called love. We like the same things. We share the same ideals and enjoy common pleasures. We momentarily forget that we are unique persons with separate identities and histories. Oh, to be alive!

In the blush of new love, ordinary men and women do things they would never do in their right minds. They are ecstatic—standing outside of themselves, as the original Greek root of that word implies—deranged or slightly mad, as bystanders judge. In this bewitched and enchanted state, many couples pledge troth and get married. Romance is the only word for this dreams-and-roses, prince-and-princess first stage of marriage. During this period, it is not so much the commitment that stands out, crucial as it is, or the mutuality and sharing, but the sweet romancing.

Romance is the total delight and abandon I experience in you. A kind of mystical union swallows us, obliterating all boundaries. Two do, indeed, become one flesh, and it feels wonderful: this is what I've always wanted and dreamed about, a love that encompasses and expands me, a love in which I give everything and receive more! This ecstacy of bliss and belonging refreshes my soul. I drink deeply; my thirst is quenched. All of creation sings the song of love. Among the articles of faith in this romantic stage is the conviction that you are the "right one," the "only one" for me. Wonder of wonders, out of all the people in the world, we met and were seized by love! Hallelujah! This marriage, surely, was made in heaven.

JOAN AND SHAWN

Joan and Shawn are overwhelmed by love. Joan first met Shawn a couple of years ago when she started a new job. It was "love at first sight" for her. However, Shawn was already married and she was adamant that she would never get involved with a married man. Though she dated many young men, she felt that none of them really met her needs or offered excitement and challenge. She openly admitted to friends that Shawn was her ideal. He had energy, drive, and stamina; he was a real go-getter who would make life exciting and rewarding.

Two years after she first met Shawn, his marriage shattered. His wife moved out, leaving him with two small children. Shawn was devastated. However, within weeks Joan managed to get close to Shawn. Then it was love at first sight for him. Joan suited him perfectly. She was energetic and sensuous and was determined to live with flair. They both enjoy classical music, going to the theater, shopping, sailing, and they could talk for hours about religions and philosophy. They spend every available moment together and are planning an early marriage. Inside, Joan just knows that "he is the one." Neither feels the need for time to help Shawn deal with his previous marriage. Neither feels the need for inner reflection or sharing about needs, desires, and historical or cultural differences. Both feel they are giving everything and receiving more. And they are sure things will always be this way.

ROMANTICISM

A sense of wonder, romance, and exclusivity does belong to marriage. Taken rightly, it has nothing to do with the myths of romanticism—that I could not have fallen in love with someone else, that I have no say in the matter, or that I must patiently wait until Mr. Right or Ms. Perfect appears. That is fatalism, a passivity that undercuts our responsibility to reach out and search for our partner in intimacy. Of course, if we are deeply insecure in our self, we can easily fall prey to such myths. Just recently a young woman, struggling to be her own person, sighed and said: "Sometimes, I just want a loving, intelligent man to sweep me off my feet and take care of me." A young man earnestly declared: "I want a woman to fall intensely in love with me so that I can feel alive. Nothing else matters."

A marriage that does not begin with a deep and mutual conviction that each person is the right one for the other and that the relationship will work is already drifting into troubled waters. In working with troubled couples married five, ten, or even twenty or more years, I often see the bitter truth surface: they knew before they got married that they were making a serious mistake, but they felt forced to marry because of sexual involvement, pregnancy, family pressure, economic uncertainties, personal inadequacies, or whatever. If people marry in spite of deep reservations (not simply normal doubts and fears), the marriage begins swamped. If the reservations are not attended to and removed, it is only a matter of time until the relationship sinks entirely.

It is far from easy to resolve such matters after the fact. If the reservations were too frightening to face in the beginning, they only become more scary as the partners build a life together. With so much at stake, there is no easy way to confess to a fear that we have made a terrible mistake; the whole thing might blow up in our faces. Instead, we push down the nagging doubts, deceive ourselves, and throw ourselves into the relationship as best we can. But a relationship begun in deception is coming apart from the start.

A second article of faith during the first stage is that powerful romantic feelings are necessary. In popular myth people are supposed to fall in love with no warning or preparation. That, of course, may happen. More commonly, young people cautiously explore relationships with various candidates until they find one where they are fairly sure the interest is mutual. Then, quite willingly and by design, they let themselves fall in love. But in this pattern too the first stage of marital love is the stage of romance.

ROMANCE AND MARRIAGE

Many marriage experts call romance the enemy of marriage. They decry romance as a selfish, irrational frenzy that raises unrealistic expectations and has little to do with married love. A companionship of respect, tolerance, and mutual advantage, not romantic love, makes, they say, for a solid marriage. Reasonable satisfaction rather than the giddiness of romance leads to a stable relationship.

With our epidemic of broken marriages, it is easy to see why romance has been singled out as the culprit. Wasn't it romance that made us lose our senses in the first place? But I believe that romance alone neither makes or breaks a marriage. And it is a cardinal mistake to pit romance against marriage. Why throw the baby out with the bathwater? One essential ingredient of a good marriage is romance—not adolescent infatuation, but the steady delight and genuine sparkle of two people who enjoy and nurture each other.

Romance is not all of married love, but it is its indispensable emotional component. Without romance, not as a constant state of arousal, but as a general feeling of comfort, pleasure, and delight, a marriage is destined to be a listless, dry, and dreary relationship, no matter how strong the commitment. Without the emotional connection we call romance, a marriage lacks the zest and excitement that lead to satisfaction. Married couples, if all is well, experience this connection in a host of unsung and un-eventful ways, as well as in the moments of intense passion, waves of tenderness, or candles and soft music. A marriage without such connection is a divorce waiting to happen.

Romance is not sexual infatuation. Romance is eros, and eros is the human drive to connection and union. "It is not good for man [or woman] to be alone." Eros is the power to move toward wholeness, a reaching out to to fulfill our deepest needs for intimacy. In our day, to be sure, the erotic has been reduced to the sexually titillating, but that is a horrible perversion of its meaning. Pornography is not erotica. Pornography has to do with isolation, violation, and dismemberment of human beings who are treated as things. Erotica has to do with intimacy, ten-derness, and yearning for the wholeness of human beings who are recognized as fellow persons.

To be sure, eros may also lead to the physical union that is intrinsic to marital intimacy. Eros is the spark that makes genital intercourse personally affirming and fulfilling. Without eros, in-tercourse is just physical stimulation and release, tumescence and detumescence. With eros, physical intercourse is human intimacy and not simply mechanical coupling.

ROMANCE AND IDENTITY

Emotional chemistry is the way most relationships start. And it's a good start—if we already have a developed sense of self. However, if we lack a sense of self, such an emotional affair can lead to real trouble. It is true that romance is good for the ego. It energizes us, making us feel more vibrant and alive. But if we lack a settled identity, romance becomes a temporary way to escape ourselves, to hide our depression, fear, and despair. Passion for the lover becomes a panacea for anemia of the ego, for loneliness, and general anxiety.

It is not romance that is the bane of marriage, but our lack of self-identity that makes us unable to cope with the power of romance. The temptation to solve our identity needs by romantic involvement is often irresistible. We can easily become so fixated on the other person, so obsessed with keeping our newly found love, that we create a fantasy world out of touch with reality.

Eventually the bubble bursts or such romance just peters out. The problem remains ourselves and the unhealthy way we used romance to bolster our sagging egos. Perhaps this is why so many of us seek extramarital affairs. When the excitement of a first-time experience wears off and becomes familiar, we need another, new adventure to lift us out of ourselves, to make us feel important and alive. Our troth relationship will have to find a more solid base than romance. But such renegotiation has to begin from the home base of self-identity. Since many of us lack such a home base or are often out of touch with it, when the relationship falters, we deny it, throw a fit, or point a finger. Often we run into someone else's arms, looking for another person to save us from facing ourselves, and so continue the cycle. Without the roots of self-identity, passion may sweep us into passivity. We allow romance to happen to us, perhaps again and again, and we become unable to make choices or keep promises.

Falling in love has more to do with us than with the other person. How we handle romance depends on the level of our own maturity. Many of us in our culture are drawn toward falling in love because we have not yet come to grips with ourselves. Finding and keeping romance alive becomes for many our very identity. If the marriage fails, we are devastated. Losing ourselves in romance is the easy way out: it seems to solve our problems, and it feels so good. What's more, its a great ego-booster and sits well with parents who want us to settle down. What we don't understand is that irresponsible romancing is skating on thin ice.

It leads to unhealthy fusion that devours both parties, until someone "escapes" into a new romantic involvement.

CORA AND BRIAN

Cora and Brian came to therapy after twenty years of marriage and two children. Cora, who had always thought of her marriage as "perfect," had just discovered that Brian was having an affair. She was bewildered and full of despair. What had happened? She thought that the two of them had shared ideals and enjoyed doing things together. She had invested everything into her roles as wife and mother. She felt they were her identity. From her ethnic background came the expectation that a woman stays home with the children. The man takes care of the physical needs of the family and provides the comforts of a middle-class way of life. This was the way of life to which she had committed herself. She was in love with Brian as much now as the day they were married. Brian and she had engaged in little introspection about their relationship and changing expectations during the years. They just coasted along.

But in the last few months, Cora had noticed changes in Brian. He seemed more outgoing, spontaneous, and in love with life. He went off to work with unusual eagerness and stayed away longer at night. He didn't seem to need her as much. He became distant and withdrawn in her presence. Their sex life had trailed off badly.

Finally, Cora got the message. Romance had gone. When she confronted Brian, he owned up. Cora became frantic, filled with terror. When her primary role cracked, she shattered. She felt her self-esteem and identity vanish. She felt empty, alone, and powerless. Who was she?

COURTSHIP: INTENTIONAL EXPLORATION OF SELF

The answer to the problems of romance is not its banishment from our lives; the answer is attention to self. Adolescent friendships are excellent ways for learning more about our likes and dislikes, our anxieties and joys, our vulnerable issues and enjoyable activities. With friends we may explore how we respond to the anxieties, strengths, and weaknesses of others. Such intentional exploration of self in relationship enhances self-awareness. Coming to sense our power, beginning to feel our space, learning our gifts and limits, we become ready to reach out for intimacy at the appropriate time. During a period of courtship, we begin to explore even more intently our reactions and responses to that particular person with whom we are romantically involved. What happens inside when she or he looks at me in a certain way? Why is my first reaction always negative? What fears do I project on my companion? Such coming to know ourselves better helps us to keep our bearings in spite of the gales of romance. This kind of courting is certainly not all tea and roses. It can be hard and painful work when two people honestly face themselves and explore their relationship. But the importance of such introspection cannot be overemphasized. Every young couple contemplating marriage is well advised to take advantage of premarriage seminars, which are becoming increasingly available. Individual counseling may offer real help to young persons in this quest for identity and intimacy. Premarital counseling can help a couple work through doubts and fears and arrive at realistic expectations.

Too many young people move directly from the dependency of the parental home to the dependency of a marital home without a chance to take a deep breath as a truly single person. But that this happens makes some sense, for when I am out of touch with myself and unsure of my power, I need an identity base for affirmation and reassurance. I don't know this is the real reason so I rationalize with others: my friends are getting married; it's adventure; I may not get another chance; Mom and Dad will be happy; now I'm a somebody.

Family and social pressures are hard to resist when I am out of touch with myself, but it's especially the inner needs that drive many of us into marriage prematurely. It's much easier to seek solace in the warmth of an embrace than to face my own cold fears head on, alone. I cultivate the illusions that my problems can be solved by someone else. And often it works . . . for a while. As I continue to push aside my dimly perceived fears and doubts, a romantic illusion usurps a healthy romance.

There are a variety of romantic illusions. In the Cinderella syndrome a woman tries to live her life through her husband. When resentments build up, she questions herself first. What's wrong with me that I don't sing the praises of this prince of a husband like everyone else does? Or the husband, under the guise of Mr. Nice Guy, avoids taking his share of the responsibility by allowing his wife to make all the decisions. He doesn't take risks, and she of course is at fault if things don't work out. She begins to feel like a mother and he responds like a child. Since the husband feels he is only trying to make her happy, he is bewildered at the growing resentment that comes his way.

TRANSITION

These kinds of dynamics lead to the second stage of marriage, which we discuss in the next chapter. All marriages that begin with romance move on to something else—usually before a year is out. Every marriage, after the romantic prelude, enters the shakedown period. But what about the marriages that begin without romance? The least that we can say is that couples who marry without a special spark between the partners will lack the deep emotional connection to sustain them in the coming winter season of their marriage. If they each have good support systems or if they have no other choice, they may stay together. But in today's society, the odds are against them, especially in urban centers where they can more easily begin new lives apart. In my experience most couples who freely choose each other begin with an initial rush of emotional energy between the partners. The attraction may have faltered and it may have been fleeting, but it was there.

ROMANCE AND ARRANGED MARRIAGES

Arranged marriages are of course a different matter. Since I'm not personally familiar with many such couples, my comments are brief and provisional. Sometimes such arrangements take place in cultures that sanction affairs of the heart outside of marriage and view marriage primarily as a domestic convenience for progeny, wealth, and social status. Yet even in such cases, although familiarity can breed contempt, it can also give rise to romance.

Romance is possible especially if the partners have a high sense of commitment to each other and to the community to which they belong. The odds for romance are also significantly enhanced when the selection process takes into consideration the personalities and interests of the partners. And as a young husband of an arranged marriage recently remarked, "Looking at the divorce statistics, I think our chances are at least as good as if we had freely chosen each other. Right now, I feel they are a whole lot better." He does make a point.

Kumar and Esmie are Indians who had never seen each other before their arranged marriage, but they "learned to love each other." They have been together for sixteen years and have three children. Arranged marriages too appear to have a romance stage; they certainly have an initial stage of excitement, novelty, and great expectations.

4. Stage Two: Power Struggle

Now wearing the costumes of man & wife
Resenting each other & not knowing why
They couldn't see the sense
They were caught up in the different
They were the typical lovers
Watching love's goodbye.

—THE PARACHUTE CLUB

In the delight of Romance, cupid pierces our hearts and we soar to heights of ecstacy. Even though the honeymoon experience may be a bit of a letdown, we feel buoyant and happy. Stage Two begins with a greening period when we begin to be impressed with our differences. Our idiosyncracies emerge. She is a morning person; he comes awake in the evening. He is a fiend about cleanliness and order; she feels most comfortable with a haphazard schedule and slight chaos. He loves company and busyness; she needs solitude and quiet. He's anxious to have a family; she's concerned about a career. She prefers the symphony; he's into movies.

ADJUSTMENT

We are into Stage Two: Power Struggle. This period of mutual adjustment with its inevitable tension is unavoidable; it's part of the marriage map. Two independent persons forming a way of life together go through a period in which adjustment to each other's ways is the primary focus. How can we do justice to each other as persons in our shared life-style? How can we form a way of troth together that honors our individual identities in an experience of deepening intimacy? Can we develop a style of intimacy that expands and liberates us rather than closes us down and restricts us as persons?

Most of us, even in our so-called open society, are inadequately prepared for coping with this period of adjustment. We have been raised in the consumer ethos of instant gratification. We are conditioned by the menus of television and advertising, of movies and magazines to expect and demand total satisfaction— now. With our heads we may know that it is myth, but it has been so programmed into our psyches that when reality serves up something less, we feel cheated, frustrated, and enraged. We deserve better. We were promised more.

For many of us there is another critical factor: lack of a firm sense of self. If we married to complete ourselves and find our identity, acknowledging differences between us is extremely difficult. When we lack a sure sense of our center and its boundaries, negotiating differences is extremely frightening. We have no inner point of orientation to separate out significant from insignificant differences. Our identity is threatened every time a difference emerges. The need to adjust seems like a demand to concede to each other. The period of adjustment turns into a power struggle.

Stage Two adjustment does not become a power struggle for every couple. Some couples may navigate this period without the intensity and turmoil of such struggle, but most couples engage in the struggle even while they remain oblivious to the underlying dynamics. Insofar as we are products of our society and insofar as we lack a solid sense of self, Stage Two is a power struggle. Since power struggle is the experience for most couples, this chapter describes Stage Two in those terms.

DIFFERENCES EMERGE

As marriage partners become aware of real differences between them, a low-grade panic sets in. Is this the person I committed myself to? Maybe I don't really know him! Does she have a secret life? I feel like an outsider! What have I gotten myself into? What am I going to do? Doesn't she know that upsets me? Sometimes I'm sure he's late just to make me mad.

Each of us takes a deep breath. Can I give him his own space? Dare I express my irritation at her? How strong am I? How strong is our bond? Questions like these mark the first big crisis in the relationship. How will we handle our differences? It's often at this time that a relationship begins to unravel. Honoring differences turns into subtle moves of attack and defense to justify our own idiosyncrasies. The partners feel unable to risk voicing their fears; that would only make things worse. She looks so happy; it must be me. He is so loving; it must be me. Each partner attempts to bury the doubt and fear for the sake of the relationship.

The crisis is very real, especially when we were sure that being in love meant no differences. When marriage is our identity, differences threaten our very being. Cross-cultural and interfaith marriages have also to cope with basic differences of marriage customs, child rearing, and religious practices. Deeply religious couples often feel a special duty to ignore and play down the emerging differences. They honestly believe that God has joined them together in the holy state of wedlock, which nothing can break. So they each put aside their growing frustration and find themselves "adapting" to the expectations of their spouse. And the pressure slowly builds. They are pleasing the other person at the cost of themselves, or resisting the other person with a sense of guilt.

Fear of facing the reality of our differences pushes us into games of denial and deceit. We put on masks and collude in establishing patterned procedures ("games") that keep the truth hidden. We rationalize: "now isn't the time to make a clean breast of our frustrations—we've just bought a house." "We're expecting a child." "I'm just imagining this anyway." "It's my fault." "I'll try harder."

Appearances can be kept up, but the nagging doubts don't go away. Little things happen; subtle changes occur. I begin to pressure my mate to be the way I want her to be. She resists, also unconsciously. She reciprocates, trying to change me into the person she wants. Small resentments take root. Slowly we retreat behind barriers and nurse our resentments. We think our spouse can't handle the truth anyway. The road of deception is slippery; once we're on it, it takes all our ingenuity to stay out of the ditch. All the while the fear lurks: "it's my fault." Slowly the stakes build. It's time to have children—the ideal solution. Having children and all the energy and work necessary to parent them can cover over the problems and keep us preoccupied for years. Likewise economic worries or family sickness can keep the issues safely hidden for long periods.

TERRY AND BERNARD

Terry and Bernard have been married nine years. For the first seven years she was completely occupied with becoming a medical doctor and he was busy building up his construction company, but the last two years have been increasingly traumatic. The tension between the two was so thick that Terry's mother left after only a two-day visit. Terry could not understand why Bernard never wanted to spend time with her. All his free time was filled with hockey, baseball, windsurfing, and squash. She was left alone at home. "At the hospital, I am respected and have a place. At home, I feel like a nobody." She brought the matter up repeatedly but each time it ended in tears. He would comfort her and tell her nothing was wrong; she was just insecure. For a long time she believed him and so she tried to fill her life with other things. They bought a new house. But nothing changed; she felt more and more empty and more and more desperate inside. She asked herself, "Do I want to spend the rest of my life unhappy?" She knew the answer was no. Finally, unable to get through to him in any other way, she refused him sex. Dragged into therapy, Bernard lamented, "Now I'm just her hot water bottle." First he insisted that he went his way only because Terry was not into sports. Then he admitted that he didn't want her along. He wanted to be free. Slowly it became clear that Bernard had projected his own deep insecurity on Terry. He had tried to run from the fact that he no longer felt connected with her—he was threatened by all the differences between them that had emerged. Afraid to admit how much he depended on her, he was withholding himself. Terry experienced his withdrawal as rejection and abandonment.

Terry and Bernard are now beginning the necessary adjustment process that follows Romance. The long struggle to finish school had hidden the problems for a long time—perhaps too long for healing. But perhaps the fire can be rekindled, for they are once again talking with each other, seeking help, and developing a new sense of themselves.

POWER STRUGGLE

Our differences need to be acknowledged and negotiated. The longer we try to postpone or detour around them, the more damaging the games become and the harder it is to escape them. Our masks become second nature to us. The questions are difficult and disturbing. What is happening? How do we resolve the conflicts? Why doesn't it just go away? Maybe it will if we just wait. Did we get married under false pretenses? The last is a touchy question, too sensitive to handle, but all our avoidance doesn't make it go away.

There is no way to avoid negotiating our differences. Yet many of us run rather than cope, stall rather than face the issues—and that's because so many of us enter a relationship without a real awareness of what is really going on in ourselves. It's not that the acknowledged reasons for our marriage turn out to be false; they continue to play their role. We marry for caring, warmth, security, sensitivity, success, excitement, money, and ambition. But few of us are sufficiently aware of what it means to make a commitment to share a life-style and a sharing, nurturing way of being in the world with another person.

NEEDED: SOLID COMMITMENT

A shared commitment in troth is of tremendous help in navigating the Power Struggle successfully. Issues can be more honestly dealt with when partners have committed themselves to endurance, openness, growth, and change. Without mutual troth, the issues that need negotiation easily become overheated. If only one partner is fully committed, he or she lives with the fear that the partner will walk out, if not always pleased. At the same time, the less-committed partner lives with guilt and is hesitant to bring up disagreements. A conspiracy of avoidance built on fear and guilt takes shape. Slowly the partners begin to resent each other and subtly make their own demands or withdrawals.

The distress exacerbates and its result may be used by either partner as the perfect excuse to leave the relationship.

A solid sense of commitment helps us hold on to each other and endure as we become more deeply aware of the underlying forces that were at work in the selection of our partner. We are often attracted to the qualities we would like to see in ourselves, but fear we do not have. We are likely to have married to complete ourselves and have chosen someone who can meet our needs. The result is a mutually attractive fit, safe and satisfying. Most often we are blissfully unaware of the emotional dovetailing that sets the basic terms of the relationship. We have little sense of the emotional trade-offs to which we have become party, and even less sense of the precariousness of the arrangement.

EMOTIONAL DOVETAILING

Choosing a marriage partner is an interplay of unconscious as well as conscious factors, and often the unconscious factors are the most important. Just as dream interpretation based on the obvious content is likely to miss the fundamental message of the dream and its depth dynamics, so attention to the most obvious reasons for choosing a partner often misses the mark.

The quality of intimacy with another is directly related to the quality of intimacy with self. Without a fairly intact ego, we cannot value another person except to the extent that he or she fulfills our own needs. Then we are simply unable to let the other person have his or her own identity or space. We need to establish control. And we are only able to satisfy our partner according to *our perception* of his or her needs, rather than according to his or her own real needs. Together we dovetail our interests so that we live off of each other. Our unconscious or subconscious needs are echoed in what we think are the needs of our partner.

The issue of control and power (who is going to control whom?) becomes the overwhelming reality to the degree that we feel powerless and helpless. The more we have a sense of our own identity and personal power the less we need to insist that we control the relationship. Then we can be vulnerable, trusting that we will be loved and our needs met. But lacking that inner assurance, we need to control to inflate our ego. Without the security that we will be loved simply for who we are, we think that we have to do something. Some of us try to force affection from the other; others try to bribe affection from the other by meeting his or her every need. In neither case do we get what we really want. When we receive such love, we feel that the other loves us because there's no other choice, or because we do everything for him or her.

When we both are driven by our fears, the power struggle begins. We seek to carve out areas over which we have control. We try to remake our partner according to our needs and desires. We use each other as bulwarks against the forces that threaten to overwhelm us. We expect our partner to provide that sense of security and well-being we lack in ourselves. Consequently, when our partner's identity needs surface and he or she insists that they be met, we move to a second line of defense. Through a series of maneuvers—manipulation is the right word—we try to remake our partner according to our specifications. If our partner resists, often trying to turn the tables on us, we move to a third line of defense and blame our partner. "You let me down." "You no longer love me." "You are selfish." "You always . . ."

CONTROL, MASKS, GAMES

Some of us seek to control by domination: we try to force our will on the other person. By possessing and controlling, we avoid our own fear of engulfment and annihilation. We inflate ourselves by incorporating another person who fears and adores us. Some of us control by submission: we allow ourselves to be pushed around, but in the process we withhold until our needs are met. By being possessed and controlled, we avoid our own fear of rejection and nonacceptance. We subtly inflate ourselves by becoming allied with a superior person who revels in our attention. Very often a dominating personality and a submissive personality are attracted to one another.

Establishing a domination/submission pattern is a survival maneuver necessary when, lacking a grounded and/or a bounded sense of self, we are driven to make a connection with another that will supply what we need. To cover our desperate need for belonging and power we put on masks that hide the reality from others and from ourselves. There are many kinds of masks: do-gooder, nice guy, know-it-all, martyr, "anything you want," "poor me," Miss Fragile, Mr. Cool, macho, sex bomb, "always good for a laugh," unreachable, and on and on.

Along with the masks come the games we play. Twenty years ago Eric Berne named and diagrammed many of these games in his *Games People Play*: IWFY (if it weren't for you), SWYMD (See what you made me do), There I Go Again (depressive), Why Does This Have to Happen to Me (paranoid), Now I've Got You, You Son of Bitch (jealous rage), Rapo (sexual revenge), Sweetheart (put down), Schlemiel (obsessive-compulsive), and many, many more.[1] How many of these secret games do we play in our relationship?

Sulking is a widespread game: if I sulk, she will feel guilty and I will get my way—just as I did with mother. Playing victim is effective: if I make myself the victim, he will rescue me and I will get attention. Becoming a persecutor so that I will become a victim so that I will be rescued is a more complicated and dangerous game of the same genre. Blackmail is a common game: you better do as I ask, or I have a headache and sex is out of the question. Withholding is a most effective ploy in the politics of power: withhold in the areas where your partner is especially vulnerable and the partner is at your mercy. The ingenuity we reveal in inventing games to keep the deception going is truly remarkable. All of us are naturally more adept at some of the games than others, especially those we learned in our childhood homes.

Underneath all the masks and games there is fear and anger, aloneness, anxiety, and despair. We use the masks and games not because we intend to be dishonest or malicious, but because we see no other way to survive. Masks help us ward off our personal demons; games anesthetize the hurt of our early traumas. Some of us adopt a basic posture of self-sufficiency and domination to hide our emptiness and fear of invasion; we remain aloof. We are "resisters." Some of us adopt the opposite posture of self-effacement and submission to hide our lack of confidence and fear of rejection; we aim to appease. We are "pleasers."

More often than not, "pleasers" gravitate toward "resisters" and "resisters" toward "pleasers." Pleasers like the self-confidence affected by the resisters; the resisters like the concern and care affected by the pleasers. The dovetailing is "perfect"—and safe. Both parties get what they want without having to risk vulnerability. "Resisters" receive attention and acceptance without having to reveal and fully invest their inner selves. "Pleasers" receive attention and acceptance without having to face their internal emptiness and fear of rejection.

JOE AND CAROL

Joe and Carol have been living together for three years. For Joe it is his second serious relationship after a marriage of ten years. For Carol, thirteen years younger, it is her first longstanding relationship. Carol is drowning. She feels that important parts of her are slowly dying. Joe can't be alone and needs sexual reassurance every night. If he doesn't get what he wants, he tells her that she doesn't love him. He tries to control her every action, is jealous of all her friends, and demands that she spend all her free time with him. She thinks she needs to leave to survive but is afraid he will fall apart. And his dad is dying.

Carol came into the relationship as a "pleaser" who knew that she would not have to fear rejection if she met Joe's needs. She now realizes that she was trying to find her identity in rescuing Joe much as she once felt called to protect and care for her father. Both Joe and her father seemed homeless and unable to care for themselves. She believed that in return for her care, she would receive affirmation as a person and be able to grow and prosper. Instead she is constantly asked to give more, and Joe can't understand her when she asks for honor and respect for the whole person she is. Isn't his need for her enough? Whenever she tries to create room for herself, he thinks she is trying to get away from him. And now she often is. So she feels guilty and gives in. But Carol is also losing her spirit—she is looking drawn and haggard; she is holding down so much hurt and anger that she is becoming tight and hard.

In therapy Carol is being encouraged to do something for herself before her spirit is devastated. She is getting in touch with her lack of self-esteem, which led her to accept a relationship she knew she could never fully commit herself to. She is beginning to find the courage to resist Joe's advances when she feels cold and distant inside. Joe is beginning to feel the crunch, so he is fighting back: "I can't give myself totally to you, because you don't make yourself totally available to me. You are the problem." Coping with the reality of two previous relationships that failed, he adds: "Maybe it will have to be another woman." Then Carol feels that he needs her only for his needs, and yet she doesn't want him to go.

One night when she is about to go out for a moment, Joe pulls out a scrap of paper with a telephone number on it. "When are you going? Then I can make a call." Suddenly Carol feels the same pain she used to feel when Joe used to call his old girl friend when he was unhappy. She shares with him what is happening. "I was only teasing. Why do you have to make such a big thing of it?" he says.

Carol is beginning to see the games they are playing. She is fighting hard to establish a new way of relating, but Joe seems unable to face the reality. He is like a bear cub that needs mother constantly around. As long as Carol gives him sex, he is content. And if she gives him sex, he can't really accept that anything is basically wrong with the relationship. If it were, she wouldn't sleep with him every night. When she refuses, Joe gets all tied up in knots, sulks, and complains. Then he is in no condition for introspection. Games can be dangerous. And unless Joe is able to own his role, it seems clear that it is only a matter of time until, for her own survival, Carol will have to leave.

DOVETAILING

Safe dovetailing is not to be mistaken for genuine intimacy. We get some of our needs met—but without having to reveal or risk our inner selves. But that is precisely why dovetailing prevents and erodes true intimacy. The partners are linked together more by their needs than by mutual openness and deep sharing. The arrangements may be convenient and rather pleasant for long stretches of time. In the sight of others they often pass for the genuine article. Indeed, we are often fooled ourselves. But if we are at all in touch with our deepest needs for self-affirmation and true intimacy, an unrest begins to smolder.

The unrest begins to gather when the underside of the dovetailing becomes apparent. Pleasers do provide care and attention for resisters, but they do it basically to obtain the care and attention that they fear will never be freely given. Resisters begin to feel the insistent demand that they had better reciprocate the care and attention. "I love you" from a pleaser is often a question: "Do you love me?" When the resisters sense that the love they receive has strings attached, their internal rage is stoked and they know again that their resistance is justified. "If I do not resist, I will be invaded." So their wariness is increased and they give even less to the relationship.

Resisters do give pleasers a sense of confidence and security, but they do it basically to obtain the security, confidence, and right to be which they lack in themselves. Pleasers begin to feel that even the slightest suggestion, challenge, or question is out of bounds. "What do you think?" from a resister is often a statement: "This is what you should think." When the pleasers sense that they are only valued when they stay in their place and do as expected, their sense of inadequacy and worthlessness is further heightened and they know again that "pleasing" will be the only way to get any of their needs met. "If I don't please, I will be rejected." At the same time, since they begin to sense that they are being used, they are less ready to give and give for fear of being engulfed.

The relationship is beginning to unravel. It's not really very safe at all! But once the system is in place, it is very difficult to change. Resisters are pressured from within and without to keep up the pretense of confidence and sufficiency. After all, that is what attracted their partners in the first place. Not only would it jeopardize their relations, it would mean facing their deep insecurity and inner loneliness. Pleasers, too, feel the pressure to keep the pretense of selfless devotion and love. That was the initial attraction that won over their partners. Moreover, it would mean facing their own need and deep inadequacy.

We fear that who we really are will not be accepted, and that fear keeps the masks on. Yet as the relationship continues, we sense internal rumblings that things are not as they seem. We begin to feel used. In quiet desperation we increase the pressure on our partner to come through or we retreat slowly into a pit of despair. The two moves usually go together. As I increase the pressure, my partner takes one step back. As I distance myself, my partner approaches. This two-step dance becomes a style of being together: in step but out of touch—negative intimacy.

Sometimes he increases the pressure by sulking to heighten his partner's feelings of guilt. And sometimes, overcome by guilt, she gives in. He takes what he can get: there may never be another chance! But the contact leaves a bitter aftertaste rather than a tender afterglow. She feels used and angry. Why can't he trust that she will reach out freely? He feels guilty and angry. Why can't she just give herself freely? In frustration both partners find ways to retaliate. But frustration and retaliation are signs of a power struggle. In themselves, they don't change the system. What we now have is a domination/submission/alienation syndrome that only heightens the tension and tightens the screws.

The submitters discover that withholding is a very effective way to counter domination. The dominator keeps pressing, the withholder withdraws even more. The distance increases and the tension escalates. The dominator may get a thrill out of forcing the partner and the submitter may feel smug in being martyred, but neither experiences intimacy. To disguise the hurt of two people whose deepest needs are unmet, a couple can easily stay locked in the struggle. Winning, not sharing, is the reality, alienation the outcome.

In the domination/submission arrangement there is a hidden flaw. Both the desire to dominate and the desire to submit are defensive postures born of weakness, not of strength. The dominator often desires, if the truth be known, to be taken care of like a little boy or little girl. The submitter is often covertly grasping for power and attention.

A teeter-totter effect sets in. If I take responsibility and dominate (as a parent), surely I have the right to expect you to "baby" me. If I please you (as a perfect child), surely I can expect to bask in your glory and enjoy doing many things my way. Instead of the equal sharing of two adults, we have two parent-child relationships that teeter-totter into their opposite child-parent relationships. Traditionally many men in our culture have acted the part of the dominant parent when, on a deeper level, they themselves have been looking for care and empathy. And women have taken on the role of submission when, on a deeper level, they have been looking for an opportunity to be somebody. It can easily be the other way around too—aggressive wives may look for tender care and submissive husbands may look for power and esteem.

The dovetailing that at first looked so safe and neat is anything but. Irritating lesions begin to appear. The "weak" partner longing for security and power feels cheated to discover that the "strong" partner is just as weak and insecure and is also, in fact, looking for an ideal, all-good parent. Likewise, the "strong" partner yearning for adulation and care feels cheated to discover that the "weak" partner is not so helpless and that the care has all kinds of strings attached. But locked in the role, a dominator is unable to own weakness for fear of rejection, just as the submitter is unable to own up to manipulation for fear of rejection. Resentments build, distances increase, and hearts close behind walls of defense.

CLARENCE AND MAXINE

Two years ago Maxine, a successful and forceful woman in her forties, married Clarence, an articulate and talented architect in his early thirties. At the time of their marriage, they also started their own business together. They had been good friends for a number of years and made a dashing couple. She carried herself with style and grace; he was suave and debonair.

Maxine brought Clarence to therapy because she was becoming very unhappy with the relationship. Clarence had no sense of time and he constantly kept her waiting. He didn't understand her, never put his stuff away, didn't take care of the dog, was drinking too much, and was walled off. Clarence quickly agreed that he was the problem and tried to make light of the whole thing in his articulate way. They talked quietly, but the room was thick with tension and unspoken threats and taunts. Even though she was aggressive and confronting, Maxine seemed cold with fear. And even though Clarence was trying to act the clown, there was hostile iciness in his eyes. They traded insults and looks but could not be vulnerable together.

After a number of weeks of individual therapy, they were able to let down some of their defenses together. Maxine was afraid that her time was running out; she feared that she was losing her beauty and her charm. Clarence no longer approached her sexually and was cold to her most seductive moves. She felt panicky. She needed his affirmation, but he continually put her down. Clarence admitted that he resented being treated like one of Maxine's possessions. "Everything at home has to be the way she wants it. What right does she have to throw out my old running shoes? She wants me to be at her beck and call. I'm her pet. I'm afraid that she'll devour me. I can't stand her disapproval; I'm afraid to say no but I can't seem to say yes anymore. I just can't satisfy her. She will always want more. I've given up."

It became clear that Clarence was underneath a very insecure little boy who looked for a mother who would give him security and love. And although Maxine was the dominant "resister," underneath she was a very fragile little girl who was desperate for Daddy's pampering. Both wanted someone to take care of them. For a while Clarence had been the "pleaser" willing to pamper Maxine to receive motherly care. For a while Maxine was willing to baby Clarence to feel rejuvenated as a woman by Clarence's youthful vitality. But as time wore on, both became hostile about the price they were being asked to pay. Each one retreated behind thick walls and began to accuse the other of not giving. She became more and more demanding. He withdrew more and more. Whenever Clarence began to soften and lower his "drawbridge," Maxine would come on like gangbusters. He would pull it up fast, and she would be left outside, humiliated, furious, and extremely vulnerable. So when Clarence was needy and approached, it would be time for her to walk the dog. And he would retreat to a corner like a beaten dog. Tit for tat.

In therapy Clarence became aware that he needed to present a smiling, confident, debonair exterior. "I need to have everything good on the outside because everything is broken inside." He had never connected with his mother. And his father, whom he adored, had left when he was five. They have not talked since. All his life he has tried to put away the deep feeling of betrayal. He would never again make himself dependent on any-one else. He can do it—will do it—on his own.

Maxine became increasingly aware that her identity was far too dependent on the sexual attention of men. Her father had pampered her but had been unable to relate to her as a person with her own desires and ideas. She had tried to take on the male model, but it left her feeling empty and unfilled underneath. She began to realize that part of her did see Clarence as a son, as a replacement for the son she had aborted some fourteen years ago. She both wanted Clarence to grow up and she didn't want him to grow up. He both wanted to remain small and be cared for and resented himself for being needy.

Clarence and Maxine developed a sense of the real issues in their lives and the way they brought out the worst in each other. They began to see that their need to control each other, Maxine as the dominant partner and Clarence as the withholder, was preventing any growth in intimacy. They decided to put their marriage on hold for a while and to try it again after each had done some work on individual issues.

BACKWARD YEARNING

If my parents, for their own reasons, overinvested or under-invested in me, my self-development has been threatened and hampered. My birth as an independent self, despite the best-intentioned efforts of my parents, has become problematic. Some births are never, in fact, completed; some parents and children are in labor all their lives. And many people, themselves not fully born, enter marriage looking for a new opportunity for deliverance. Thus, my search for a partner can be driven more by a lingering desire to recover my parental home than by a desire to make a new home for myself. I yearn more for a re-union with my parents than for a new union with another person. How could it be otherwise when, not intact myself as a person, I need marriage to attain rather than to give self. This backward yearning is an attempt to recapture what is necessary to heal the old hurts. Locked into the past, I attempt to remake my partner into the perfect parent. Then, something in my psyche urges, all will be well with my soul.[2]

But there is even more involved. In our search to recapture the past we find ourselves irresistibly attracted to a partner who is basically, if not externally, very much like (or very much unlike) our parents or other significant nurturer. I will describe the dynamics by using the example of an overinvesting, intrusive nurturer, but the same pattern emerges, other things being equal, in the case of an underinvesting, distant nurturer. Even if everything in me wants to run from an all-consuming mother, for example, I may be drawn to a partner who exhibits the same urge to overwhelm because of its familiarity. My emotional dials are superactivated—I feel alive, even if on guard. Even though I sense its danger, I feel myself irresistibly drawn in. Maybe this time the connection will be good. Thus, even though I long for deliverance from my earliest conflicts, I am well on the way to reenacting them. Or, in an effort to avoid an intrusive mother, I may be drawn to a partner who keeps a safe distance. But when my partner doesn't give me the attention I need and demand (because of his or her own fear of intimacy) I feel disconnected, cheated, and alone. The relationship does not satisfy. I have escaped reenactment, but since I have not received the love and care I need, the early hurt remains. But whatever route I take, I remain stuck. Catch-22!

No wonder the pain cuts so deep when I realize that the marriage isn't working. I am just repeating the original trauma once again. In fear and desperation I may hit out at my partner, or I may withdraw even further, or I run and run, or...

The sad truth is that tailoring my marriage to meet my own unresolved needs entangles me in another person's needs. We do not really meet as free persons: we marry into our weaknesses rather than our strengths. And the more we blame the other person rather than look at self, the more we are unable to give as equals in mutual intimacy. We never feel so much alone as when we are together. We feel orphaned once more, sentenced to walk the corridors of life alone.

A SEEMING TRUCE

Even when we sense the problems, even when our hearts are anguished, it is terribly difficult to face the truth. We have so much at stake, so many years, so much energy put into it. It feels like a no-win situation. If we don't face reality, our relationship will slowly disappear in a grey fog or get trampled in battle; if we do, our relationship may blow up in our faces. But facing reality means facing ourselves, our complicity, and our failure.

Somewhere in the course of the power struggle, most couples seek a way out. They strike a truce of sorts. Realizing that something needs to happen, they pull back, agree to be more considerate, more communicative, less selfish—we all know the lines. The couple agrees to a cessation of hostilities, a standoff with no winners and, they hope, no losers.

However, an agreement to try harder and be more loving— without inner reflection, growth, and change—is only an interim solution. For a while there is relief. The couple may turn to family, careers, friends, church, and social projects. But a cessation of hostilities is a far cry from intimacy. The truce is uneasy because lack of passionate involvement slides almost imperceptibly into absence.

Being absent in spirit while present in body is a tiring, sad, and deeply alienating experience. The affirmation we miss and the gaping dissatisfaction we feel eats away inside, ulcerating the spirit. Our lives become dull, heavy, and joyless. We may plunge frantically into externals to forget ourselves and fill the void, but the internal pain, unless we totally numb ourselves, can only be ignored so long.

THE TRUCE BREAKS

For most couples, especially in an urban setting where the social pressure to stay together is less intense and where the possibilities of starting anew are much greater, a truce cannot last. We simply cannot keep our deepest needs for intimacy submerged. Under the cover of the truce, unattended hurts slowly breed deep hostilities and we stockpile our arsenal of resentments.

Then one day the thin ice of the truce breaks. Usually there is a triggering event or series of events that leads to a renewal of hostilities. It may be the shock of death, sickness, or loss of a job. It may be as momentous as an affair or as trivial as a look in the mirror. Whatever, life is never the same again. We realize that change is unavoidable. Maybe not right now, but soon. The negativity that has developed threatens to swamp our marriage.

This is a scary time in any marriage. The truce didn't work. The safe dovetailing has not led to inner connection and intimacy. The impasse needs to be broken: I need my partner to understand and affirm my selfhood. The loneliness and alienation is no longer bearable. In response one partner tends to parry and thrust, defend and countercharge, resist intrusion and demand entrance. Under constant attack, the other partner begins to lose a sense of self and retreats even further. Frustration and alienation continue to build; the relationship continues to erode.

Not every marriage, of course, breaks out in physical violence or high-powered shouting matches. Some do, as the high incidence of battered wives, husbands, and children reminds us. But after the period of a relative truce, marriages do get embroiled in another round of deep and more open conflict. One or both of the partners are no longer able or willing to hide their deep dissatisfaction. The conflict ensues along the old lines. Some spouses, usually the dominant ones, attempt to reassert their control and force compliance. They attempt to retrench in the old pattern, in effect denying the seriousness of the situation. If that doesn't work, they may rant and rave to drive their partners into submission. They are deeply fearful that any change will undermine their dominant position. Some spouses, often the submissive ones, attempt to find independence and self-esteem outside the relationship. If that doesn't force a change in attitude, they may end up leaving.

Underneath all the maneuvers there is a growing inner desperation: will I ever feel affirmed and accepted for what I am by you? Will I ever be able to let down my guard and open my heart to you? Is there no relief from the prison of my loneliness? The anguish of the struggle can be unbearable. A final scream erupts from my deepest being: "Why won't you affirm and accept me for the person I am? Why? Why?"

Our deepest identity needs can no longer lie unfulfilled. The final plea for affirmation and acceptance can come out as a full-

throated cry or as an inarticulate groan; it can be a silent withdrawal or a stinging attack. But the message is the same. Often
we may not be consciously aware of the depth of our cry. Sometimes our cry for acceptance is disguised in relentless attacks to
break down our partner's defenses. Sometimes only the sigh of
defeat signals the reality. Not fully cognizant of what we are
really asking for, it's doubly difficult to hear our partner's cry.

CONFRONTATION AND BREAKTHROUGH

The deep yearning for affirmation and acceptance leads to a
time of intense crisis for the partners. We may not sense the
depth of the issues, but we do know that something needs to
happen if we are to continue together and grow. We realize in-
tuitively that the old ways of being together won't work any longer. The erosion of our relationship must be stopped before it's
too late. Together we face the ultimate test: can we turn our
relationship into a connection that nourishes rather than throt-
tles our spirits?

We sense the need to honestly face our situation, for our commitment is slowly dying. Sometimes partners continue to "hang
on" to each other, but it is more out of dogged determination
than joyful desire. In any case, unless something happens, even
if the marriage does not die, something dies inside our souls. So
we begin to look for ways to bring the issues into the open. Some
of us deliberately choose the occasion, others find themselves
suddenly revealing their deepest feelings without planning to.
The truth may come out in quiet statements or in torrents of
anger and tears. It may come out all at once or over a period
of time. But we both know that it is the truth—and that is the
crucial factor. Such sharing from the heart forges a connection.
We open our hearts to each other. We begin to take off our
masks; we lower our defenses; layer by layer we reveal our inner
selves. Not all at once, but a beginning is made. Two hearts in
the communion of openness is a mystery beyond words, a connection that fills our souls with gladness. It is good! Simple and
profound, disarming and difficult, food for the soul. Giving and
receiving the truth, we give and receive ourselves.

In the mystery of such sharing, something breaks through. In searching for understanding and love from you, I realize, in the flash of paradox, that first of all I need to accept myself! That turn inward to self-discovery has as many scripts as there are people to live them, but they are only variations on a common theme: my deep need for acceptance from you is at the same time my need for self-acceptance. Instead of projecting my needs on you, I begin to turn inward and face myself. It was my own lack of self-confidence and self-acceptance that drove me to avoid or pressure you. I needed you to make me happy because I was deeply unhappy. I needed your acceptance in overblown ways to convince me that I was acceptable. I needed to force affirmation from you because I lacked a sense of my own worth. I pointed the finger at you to avoid facing my own feelings of inadequacy and guilt. I tried to remake you into an ideal parent who would love me because I felt unlovable. If only you would love me, my emptiness would be filled and my fearful heart would be stilled. Too often I saw you as a means to my ends. Closed in on myself, I was unable to be open-hearted with you and honor you as a separate person.

It is in the self-discovery of such meetings that we rediscover each other in deeper intimacy. Accepting more profoundly my fears and needs, owning my games and masks as defenses against intimacy, learning to let myself be as the gifted and limited person I am opens the way to discovery of you as you are. Recovery of intimacy with self is at the same time preparation for enriched intimacy with a partner. My coming clean and facing myself invites you to do the same. Our commitment deepens.

Experiencing my honesty, understanding, and self-revealing openness, you are surprised and deeply touched. Openness invites openness. You too are moved to open your heart in the mutuality of troth. You may not be able to open right away or completely—you may be too blocked, too frightened, or too hurt yet—but a beginning has been made. When we are able to face our inner selves and realize our defenses and projections, the way is clear for our relating as persons in our own right, each owning our own needs, fears, and strengths. The way is open to intimacy.

TIME OF DECISION

The breakthrough may happen suddenly in a number of highly charged meetings, or it may take effect gradually, over a longer period of time. In any case, our commitment is deepened and affirmed. The relationship moves on to Stage Three. Unfortunately this sorting out does not always end in mutual self-discovery and renewed intimacy. For some couples, one or both of the partners are too blocked, too frightened, or too hurt. Sometimes they feed on each other's fears until they feel even more lost together. The intense interaction may bring on a sense of panic that they, like two swimmers in distress, are pulling each other down into the murky depths. Or sometimes only one of the partners is able to crawl out from behind the defenses. The other partner remains ensconced behind a series of barricades.

In any case, it is during the last phase of Power Struggle that a decision becomes inevitable. In the final analysis, are we, despite our problems, good for each other and is our relationship worth maintaining? Yes or no? If no, do we settle for less or do we separate? If yes, do we accept our relationship fundamentally as it is or do we commit ourselves to the process of forging new ways of being together with the purpose of deepening the intimacy? The questions are as important as they are complex and difficult.

SETTLING FOR LESS

In our society, each of the four options is possible and each of them appears well represented. Sometimes we back off from confronting and resolving the basic issues between us and settle for less even when we know the high cost of doing so. Some couples prefer a reasonable coexistence with a minimum of pain and conflict because the risk and uncertainty that comes with facing the hard realities is too much for them to bear. Opting for a new way is a voyage into the unknown. Better a bird in the hand, than ten in the bush. Engrossed in raising a family or furthering careers, they settle for an arrangement that is relatively free from daggers and wounds, even though it is not the joyful and affirming relationship they desire.

Although such marriages seem more endured than enjoyed, some seem to manage for a lifetime without any outright explosion. Some couples persevere for a lifetime because of their commitment to the indissolubility of marriage. Others stay together for the sake of the children or because they cannot risk losing their position in the community or the comforts they have worked for over a period of many years. Some couples resign themselves to unexciting futures because they simply see no other possibility. Those couples who place more value on satisfying external needs than internal needs seem to be best able to endure a settle-for-less arrangement. There are even many "couples"—sometimes called "married singles"—who live totally beside each other sharing only a common address. They separate without officially separating. And some people stay in their marriages and try to compensate by having another relationship on the side.

Whatever the details, a settle-for-less marriage remains uneasy because of the unresolved questions that remain. The danger is that when the problems can no longer be avoided in their full force, too much hurt and rancor has built up to repair the relationship. Today we hear more and more often of long-term marriages breaking up because one or both of the partners are no longer able to live with a relationship that is deeply flawed. This is especially the case when people in their forties and fifties cannot bear the thought of spending the rest of their lives in an unhappy alliance.

UNSPOKEN ACCEPTANCE

Settling for less is one alternative; we all know couples who have made that choice. At the same time we all know couples who *seem* to have settled for less because there seems to be little or no depth of intimacy expressed in the relationship, yet they exhibit a deep sense of acceptance of one another and regard their marriage as basically good. For them the question of staying together or separating is not even a genuine question. They are committed to each other and will continue to be together. Their mind-set and reality-experience know no other way. They are often unable to comprehend the fact that some couples cannot make it together. They think of broken marriages as an alien reality that need not be.

Knowing such couples makes us stop and think. This type of marriage is not easy to describe because the partners seem to spend little time reflecting on their marriage, preferring to get on with the business of marriage and family. Such couples seldom come for therapy and only rarely do they enroll in marriage enrichment courses. The few I have had occasion to talk with in my seminars profess to have a good marriage but are unable to say much about it. In fact, they have a hard time relating to the question. They seem to handle each problem as it comes with little attention to their internal feelings and yearnings. They are largely oblivious to the character structure issues that limit their intimacy. But even though they often appear to have a limited sense of self-identity and a limited ability to express intimacy, they do give evidence of mutual acceptance. In many cases there is an intense dependency relationship, a kind of fused identity they take for granted.

It seems that these couples have not chosen the settle-for-less option. It is true, looked at from the vantage point of those who have rather highly developed inner lives and a developing capacity for deep intimacy, these marriages seem to miss a certain depth of intimacy. But this does not bother those in marriages of this kind; they accept each other and appear basically satisfied with their arrangement. This is their way of relating; they do not feel that they are settling for less. They accept what is enriching and find other persons and situations to fulfill parts of themselves that cannot be fulfilled in their marital relationship. On the other hand, those who settle for less *know* that they are settling for less.

At the same time, in our culture with its growing emphasis on intimacy and identity, I would expect that in the future fewer and fewer people will be able to accept a relationship that lacks deep and free sharing of inner selves. The more we work through the meanings of our character structures, take off our masks, and reveal our deepest yearnings, the more sensitive we are to our deep need for connection with our partner. On the other hand, the less both partners are given to introspection, the more likely they may experience their marriage as satisfying even if there is not a very deep level of intimacy. The more we tend to live externally, the less we will miss deep connection with another person. In such cases, when couples basically meet each other's nurturance needs, they expect no more. They don't seem to miss the deep mutual sharing of heart-to-heart intimacy.

But experience tells me that sometimes couples act and live as if they were basically at ease with each other when in fact they harbor deep unresolved hurts or nurse secret grudges within their souls. All of us owe it to ourselves and to our partner to be completely honest with each other on this fundamental level. If we are not, we risk letting the unattended issues build up until our relationship suddenly explodes. Sometimes new experiences awaken deeply buried yearnings and hurts of which we were not even consciously aware. Then to continue to pretend that all is well is playing with fire. Listening to, expressing, and attending to our internal sounds is important preventive medicine for good relations. The moral of all of this is simple, but crucial: if our marriage is untroubled, great; but if we do have problems, we must deal with them—now—before they get so big that they are overwhelming.

SEPARATION

Separation is another choice many couples prefer when the partners sense the depth of the differences between them. They don't know what else to do. The pain seems too much, or the fear is too great. Often they lack a support network that can help them work on the problems. Sometimes someone leaves without explanation and without goodbyes. But separation without facing the fundamental issues and without concerted efforts to develop a new way of being together is very problematic. In effect it is trying to solve a problem by running away from it. But when we run, we always take ourselves along, and we are part of the problem. Sometime, sooner or later, we will have to face our share in the failure if we are to find deep healing in our lives. Leaving without a full airing of the problems over a period of time leaves a host of haunting, unanswered questions for both parties. Unless at a latter date they avail themselves of separation counseling, they deprive themselves of the painful but necessary process of disentanglement.

To leave your partner after one, ten, or twenty years without struggling hard to save the marriage can be particularly damaging. In such situations it often takes years, especially for the abandoned spouses, to come to grips with the separation. Some people never recover. Emotional entanglement does not end with physical distancing. Even involvement with another person does not undo the tie. The process of separation with its anguish and despair cannot be detoured or cut short. If the persons involved are going to be emotionally free to go on with their lives and seek genuine intimacy, they need to work through the reality of the breakup and acknowledge their part in it. When our marriage has failed, we need to know what we contributed to the breakup; we need to know how we dovetailed in safe but ultimately alienating ways and where our needs got the best of us. We need to let out the anger and the hurt; we need to mourn the loss and grieve before we can let go and say goodbye. We need to admit that we failed, repent of our shortcomings, and ask for forgiveness.

The process of separation is wrenching and bewildering at any time, but it is doubly hard if the partners part before they have struggled intensely with the whys and wherefores of their breakup. Short of that, they will most likely go on to repeat the old pattern with another person. If the process of disentanglement is avoided or prematurely halted, the couple frequently remains emotionally intertwined for the rest of their lives. Many find themselves unable to give themselves to a new relationship. Others frantically try to recreate the first marriage with a second or even third partner. They will do anything but admit that their first big love affair failed and continue to pursue the perfect partner made in the image (or anti-image) of the first spouse. Without a genuine coming to grips with what went wrong, the chances are very high that all subsequent relationships will bog down in the same dynamics that swamped the first relationship. I still vividly remember the look that came over a man as he blurted out: "That's the same bind I was in with my first wife!" For these reasons joint counseling is highly recommended for a couple even if they are adamant that the marriage is over.

STRUGGLING AND GROWING TOGETHER

The most satisfying and growth-promoting choice is choosing to stick with the process and developing new and healthier ways of being together. Not that the process is easy. Nevertheless, it can be the way to a deeply affirming relationship. The rewards for self and marriage when the passage is successfully negotiated make it all worthwhile. Some couples can negotiate the narrows of Stage Two without therapeutic assistance, but for many of us the struggle is so subtle, the fear and inner anger so intense, the lack of support from the extended family or friends unavailable or disheartening, that we need special help and guidance in finding our way through the threatening reefs and shimmering sandbars. We may need to be renurtured as individuals to achieve a more wholesome sense of self, which in turn empowers us to more fully honor each other as persons. Some of us may especially benefit from support groups, marriage enrichment seminars, or marital therapy.

Therapy, whether individual or marital, is not magic. We have to find our own way, but a competent therapist can act as a guide to accompany us through the narrows, alert us to dangers, and warn us about hidden reefs. He or she can help us face the fearful ghosts of the past and be with us in the pain of the internal journey of self-discovery.

However, even when both partners give themselves to the process and are willing to work hard on the relationship, there is no guarantee that intimacy will flourish. The fear that the marriage may not work is, in fact, one of the major reasons why we avoid facing the underlying issues for so long. Sometimes there is too much pain, too much hurt. Sometimes the partners discover that there never was a deep inner connection but only a collusion of needs, or they realize that together they are slowly but surely destroying each other. Separation may be the only healing alternative.

Although separation is always surrounded by anguish and distress, when separation comes *after* a process of deep struggle it has a different quality about it than separation *before* such a process. As we have just noted, separation before such a struggle is premature. People often wonder for the rest of their life if things could have been different if they had done this or that. If separation occurs after trying this and that and the next thing, they know with more certainty that the relationship wasn't to be, despite their best intentions. They are more easily able to let the brokenness be, let go, and move on to new beginnings.

KATHERINE AND MORRIS

Katherine and Morris came for therapy after being married for twenty years because they were "desperate." The only good thing about their relationship was sex. And that was also the only thing they agreed about. Katherine was alert, composed, and articulate; Morris was quiet, guarded, and resigned. Katherine had a litany of complaints: Morris was irresponsible and incompetent; he couldn't carry on an intellectual conversation and always watched television. She didn't respect him and couldn't trust him. When it was Morris's turn, he would no sooner get a sentence out than she would take over. Morris tried for a while, but then he backed off. Katherine took after him. Finally he told her to shut up for a change. She burst into tears. He said that he was sorry. That sequence turned out to typify their relationship.

Katherine considered herself the responsible one. Consequently she never trusted Morris nor respected his space or ideas. Morris felt emasculated, so he retreated—until it would get too much and then in rage he would pack his bags. Morris's rage in turn paralyzed Katherine. It reminded her of father's drunken anger. Terrified of being abandoned, she did anything to appease Morris. Katherine browbeats and blames; Morris retreats and sulks. Then there's a big scene and the cycle begins all over.

Underneath her hard exterior, Katherine has a soft, tender side that is crying for affirmation and love. She seldom shows it to Morris because she is afraid that he will take advantage of it. She tries to hide it from herself because it hurts too much. Her fear of abandonment keeps her in the unhappy marriage. Underneath his laid-back style, Morris is a tender but hurt soul. He has a hard time being vulnerable with Katherine, because he fears it will be a repeat of the squelching he experienced at home from his mother.

Morris is afraid of Katherine. He is sure that she thinks their marriage was a big mistake and that the only reason she married was out of guilt because of their premarital sex. Katherine is afraid that Morris is not really committed to her. She does think the marriage was a mistake, but it took her twenty years to admit it. To hide her misgivings and erase her guilt she was determined to make him into someone that she could respect. It hasn't worked. Morris realizes that he has little sense of self. He remarked, "I really don't know what it means to be *personally* committed to you." Katherine immediately jumped all over him: "See, I knew that I couldn't count on you." However, when Morris said that he would leave right now if he had the strength, Katherine's own deep insecurity surfaced and she panicked.

Gradually, over the period of a year and a half, they were able to be more open and honest with each other. Morris admitted to being involved with other women during the last years. Katherine was able to show more of her tender self. At times it looked as if there was a chance for reconciliation. But one day Morris left. He couldn't take it anymore. The mere sight of Katherine continued to make him feel like a bumbling idiot. Katherine was deeply hurt and angered; it was her worst fear realized. Slowly they have been making new lives for themselves. Morris feels that he has been let out of prison. Katherine is owning her own power and realizing that she can make it on her own. And for the first time in her life the word "happy" is not just a word.

NEEDED: MARRIAGE TUNE-UPS

In the end, there is no guarantee for the success of a marriage. In the end, each couple faces the decision of whether the relationship is worth maintaining. For some, the question is not very real and its answer obvious: we stay together. For many others the question is as real as it is sensitive. But for all of us marrieds—especially if we're in Stage Two—it is important that we periodically give focused attention to the state of our union. We have six-month dental checkups and year-end stock appraisals, yet we often hesitate to give the same attention to our marriage. When something is wrong, it only gets worse through inattention; we know that about machines but forget that it holds true in relationships. We need to accept this simple truth—and act on it. Many of us take our cars in for tune-ups at the first sign of trouble, but never dream of seeking help for our marriages until they are shambles. Marriages can get to that critical juncture beyond which repair is almost impossible.

All couples, even those who are certain of the stability of their relationship, need to take time each week to share the inner perceptions and experiences of the past week. I say this with some urgency. As I was writing these words, the telephone rang. It was a young woman in tears. Her husband of four years had just told her that the marriage wasn't working and that he wasn't coming back. "I can't believe it. I was happy. I was looking forward to the best year of our lives." However, after a few minutes conversation, she "remembered" that he had seemed rather distant during the last year and he had decided to work out of town all summer. But she had told herself it was the press of his studies and lack of a good job opportunity in their home town. We arranged for a therapy session, but he refused to come: "It won't do any good. It's over." Her last words still ring in my ears: "But I need to know what went wrong. How can I get on with my life if I don't know what happened? What did I do wrong?"

Perhaps it's not too late to help this couple, but it seems doubtful. The problems festered unattended for too long. Just because we ourselves think our relationship is in good shape is no guarantee that it is; we need to check it out with our partner. The story of this young woman is not an isolated example. The event of one partner suddenly leaving without notice after even twenty or more years of marriage is far from uncommon. And often the "left" partner is shocked and devastated: "I thought we had a pretty good marriage."

Intimacy and troth cannot be taken for granted. They are tender plants in need of constant and loving care. We owe it to each other and to ourselves—as a sign of our troth—to seek help when we need it. In Chapter 8 we will return to this subject. Now we need to know that with a solid sense of commitment and caring support and help, we can pass through the narrows of Power Struggle and begin to shape new ways of being together that strengthen the bond of love. That is what the next stage—Shifting Gears—is all about.

5. Stage Three: Shifting Gears

Facing each other's pain
Choosing to try again
Talking about new values
Building up confidence
Sexual Intelligence
On the way to self-respect
They were just a typical people
No longer in a myth.

—THE PARACHUTE CLUB

Stage Three is a breath of fresh air. It's light at the end of the tunnel for couples who have stayed together through the perilous passage of Stage Two. Nothing is the same anymore, even as they face the same realities of life together. Each sees the same faces on the other, winces at the same irritating habits, but something is changing—for the better. Fear of the unknown crops up, a what's-going-on feeling, but the happy side of that is a sense of openness, acceptance, and willingness to change. Moods of exhilaration alternate with twinges of guilt and attacks of fright. It's a strange time, a time of new growth and development as the partners learn to know each other in new ways. When we see each other as independent people and not as appendages, it becomes a tender time. With respect and awe we develop a whole new style of being together. There are times of pain when we realize that we have fallen back into old patterns, times of joy when we experience release from ways of reacting that have held us in bondage for so long. Above all, it's a period of revived hope.

LOOKING INWARD

Stage Three is the spring of promise that follows the winter of discontent. Stage Three is the dramatic growth that comes when frozen hearts melt and pour themselves out to one another in the spirit of acceptance. The relationship acquires a new depth that lifts the spirits. The shift to a more healthy way of being together begins when the partners desist from habitually looking outward at each other as the source of the problems and begin to look inward at themselves, owning their own responsibility. We give up the illusion that our partner needs to make us happy and we relinquish our insistence that he or she make it right. That is immeasurably more difficult than it sounds.

Covering up my own inadequacies by pointing the finger of blame at my partner is a survival mechanism that exists in many forms, hidden and blatant. Peering at the mote in our partner's eye blinds us to the beam in our own eye. We have heard "It's the woman" or "It's the man" since the Fall of our first parents. The healthy shift begins when we stop projecting on others and start looking at ourselves. It's often not a nice picture. There is reason after all for our fear of self-knowledge. When I begin to look inward at my motives and excuses, at my games and masks, I run right into my own deep fears and hidden angers. I despair as I lower myself into my deepest pain. I own my intense anger. I come across sensitive spots that I had closed myself off to; I open doors in myself that I never knew were there. But out of the darkness of letting pain be pain, I slowly am able to let go of the hurt, anger, and despair.

The route of self-knowledge is always a route through fear, anger, and despair, but it is a way to personal power, inner peace, and the ability to love and be loved. There are general charts and guides for the journey, but each of us must make it ourselves; no one can do it for us. It's often a slow, long, and arduous process, but self-discovery has its own unique and inimitable joys. And even though it's a long process and we may become discouraged at times about our lack of progress, the gains far outweigh the sorrows. I come to realize that I really don't need a parent figure to take care of me and make everything right. I am a person in my own right, with power and ability to act on my own. True, when I was a very small infant, I needed someone to make it all better. Even when I was a toddler, mother's kiss was the magic ointment to heal my scraped knee and hurt ego. But now I am an adult with the power and ability to act on my own.

The process of no longer projecting on others means coming to terms with our unresolved issues from our early childhood years. We need to face our own inner struggles, the power of our particular family system, and the influences of our cultural background. For until we come to grips with our early experience, family, and tradition, we remain prisoners of their power. Emotionally we remain young children. Learning to deal with our past hurts and the illusions we've created to spare ourselves suffering is a difficult journey. The illusions have become second nature to us. We live by them. To give them up, even if it is the road to a deeper life, may feel at low points like dying. But unless we turn inward instead of pointing the finger outward, we run the real risk of killing our own spirit or the spirit of a loved one.

In risking the journey inward, seeking wholeness and healing, we will not avoid suffering. But in and through the pain we come more and more in touch with ourselves. Perhaps the worst condition is one in which we are so lost in our masks and games that we are no longer conscious of being absent from ourselves. Happy is the person who recognizes and experiences unhappiness, who can really be unhappy and not merely limp. Facing our hurts is a tough assignment, but it is a necessary one, because, unattended, they continue to suck the joy out of living. The pain is not easy to bear, but it is a sign of life. And, if we can avoid numbing ourselves against the pain, it can lead us to face the issues. It's a nudge in the direction of healing.

Letting pain be pain releases new energies to move in and through pain to new life.[1] I discover in myself a power to love, to give, and to create. I begin to accept myself in my strengths and weaknesses. I begin to know myself in new and deeper ways. Reconnecting with self, I am in a good position to connect in more healthy ways with others. No longer seeking my anchor in another person, no longer demanding that someone else make me happy, I am ready to reach out to others without strings attached. Growing in self-presence, I can grow in my presence to others. My shaky self-esteem begins to firm up. Confidence seeps into my being—not all at once or all the time, but nevertheless, it's beginning. Now is the springtime of the soul.

There are times, of course, when we find ourselves caught on the old treadmills, playing the same old tunes, engaging in the familiar games of defense and attack. Just when we thought we were through the worst, we spiral downward and reenact the old scripts once more. That, however, is the nature of human growth—a spiral movement forward that includes some movement backward.

The vulnerability and tentativeness of new life cry out for personal support networks. Giving up an unhealthy leaning on our partner is easier said than done. We need a lot of support. Often it is best received from friends, support groups, or caring therapists and counselors. We may grow in confidence as we develop new skills. Often our primary partner is so involved in his or her own growth that it is most difficult for him or her (as for us) to give wholehearted support without some of the old strings attached. In the spiral process of self-growth, with adequate support, I slowly connect with myself in new ways and discover that I am growing in my ability to make more solid connections with others. Fearful and tentative but still genuine giving and receiving replaces the more customary taking and demanding. More grounded in myself, I discover that I need not be so afraid of being close to someone else. Discovering that I can indeed live with myself slowly acts to dissolve my obsession that I need someone else to provide the assurance that I am lovable and can love.

What happens on such inward journeys far outstrips my ability with words. They have to be experienced. But when it happens you know that something profound is taking place in your life. Transforming experiences speak for themselves.[2]

THE SHIFT TO A NEW WAY OF BEING TOGETHER

A major shift in the marriage relationship begins with a radical look at ourselves. When we come to grips with the full extent of how we contribute to the problems and cease projecting on our partner, a different and potentially more fulfilling and equal relationship is possible. But since any relationship involves two people, it takes willingness on the part of both to look at their roles. If one of the partners continues to plead innocence or is adamant in refusing to acknowledge that anything is wrong, the relationship as a whole remains stymied and the partners frustrated. This can happen especially when one of the partners sees his or her cultural or religious tradition, family background, or gender as "superior" or the norm.

But when both of the partners face themselves, their fears and defenses, their projections and hurts, they are also able to face their complicity in their marriage. Healing begins when each of the partners acknowledges the contribution he or she makes to the stalemate. Together we begin to acknowledge the games we play and the reasons we play them. Together we take off our masks, revealing hidden fears, inner despairs, and smouldering angers. We confess guilt. Relief is tangible as our partner hears that we are as much of the problem as she or he is. We begin to discuss and understand the ways we emotionally dovetail, the ways we are good and bad for each other, the deeper reasons why certain actions or phrases cause us to flare up or withdraw. We share the ways each of us contributes to the symbiosis. How do we consciously or unconsciously sabotage our partner's move to independence? How do we undermine moves to get close?

We begin to share our inmost fears and let each other in on our wildest dreams. We let each other know where we are and what we are feeling. We commune and share, talking with each other rather than to each other or about each other. We begin to let each other know about things that really matter, things that especially trigger negative reactions on our part. We become sensitive to situations that can easily set us off and take pains to avoid overreacting. We try to avoid ways of being that we know are painful to our partner. We learn to admit that our partner is right when they catch us indulging in our favorite defensive games. We risk being honestly angry with our partner rather than let the situation heat up in the old ways.

Miracles of miracles, as we learn to accept ourselves, the good and the bad, we find ourselves increasingly able to accept others for the persons they are with both their negative and positive qualities. It is hard to overemphasize the importance of developing a view of self that neither papers over the bad nor exaggerates the good. For unless we are able to accept good and bad in ourselves, we have difficulty in accepting good and bad in others. Unless we can accept good and bad in the same person, we are emotionally predisposed to divide the world into the good and the bad. For some people this means an oscillation between believing they are the greatest to fearing they are the worst. Others consistently see themselves as God's gift to the world or the lowest of the low. Whatever the case, an all-good/all-bad dichotomy makes living together extremely difficult, if not impossible, for we turn our partner into the all-good or all-bad and are unable to respond to him or her as a whole person.

A self-acceptance that includes the positive and the negative releases us from the need to turn our partner into an ideal father or mother as a substitute for a poor connection in the past. Nor do we need to make our spouse into an all-bad mother or father in an effort to recreate our early scripts and provide an outlet for our seething rage. Present to self and accepting of self, we can be available to the other and see that person as he or she is without insisting that person be what we want him or her to be. A positive growth spiral develops. Having listened to our own internal sounds, we can listen to the life sounds of the other. Feeling heard, accepted, and affirmed, the other person reaches out to us, hearing and affirming us as the person we are. In the mutual listening we discover each other's uniqueness and experience personal affirmation. Personally affirmed, we are encouraged to reach out and are able to yield to each other's needs.

MURRAY AND DAPHNE

Daphne came to therapy because of fears that she was slowly losing herself. Her marriage with Murray was good on many levels. "We're good friends," was her comment, but she felt that there was no zing or zest in their relationship. They seldom had sex, but she felt like a bad girl to ask for it. She wanted inner contact with him. Outwardly everything was fine: "I've always said that I could manage." But she was beginning to have hallucinatory-like experiences in which a "malevolent evil entity" pursued her and she would find herself crying because of intense feelings that she wanted what she shouldn't have. She needed more out of her marriage but felt unworthy. Why couldn't she accept what she had? Murray seemed happy enough.

Encouraged and supported, Daphne was able to tell Murray her fears and hopes. She whispered that she couldn't take it anymore. Something had to change or she feared that she would go mad. Initially Murray, a successful computer executive, just sat like a stone and listened. "I didn't realize anything was wrong." But suddenly he broke down, crying, "I know. I know. I'm afraid to come close to you." He said that his mother had overwhelmed him, demanding everything of him. Inside he felt that Daphne would drain him too, so he had to keep a safe distance. Never before having heard anything but praise for his mother, Daphne was deeply touched. The conspiracy of silence was broken. Murray confessed to wanting more too but was afraid it was his fault. He felt sexually inadequate.

It is a common occurrence for both partners to keep silent because each of them is sure that he or she is the problem. When Murray and Daphne pulled off their masks, their relationship came alive. They were able to look each other in the eye. Daphne saw Murray in a new light. He did have feelings and was vulnerable. In fact, Daphne went into shock for a period. She wanted to take it all back: "Poor Murray. I have no right to do this to him." At the same time, she wanted to run because he reminded her of her father whom she pitied.

Slowly Daphne became able to stay with her feelings, both owning her anger that Murray wasn't there for her and acknowledging her fear that she had nothing to give him. She began to realize that by not dealing with her inner feelings and needs, she was slowly killing herself under the illusion that Murray couldn't stand the truth. For his part, Murray was able to admit that he lived most of his life in his head, repressing his love-hate relationship with his mother and his anger at his alcoholic father who was never there. Both Daphne and Murray have begun to look at their own projections, patterns, and games. They are committed to facing the deeper issues. Murray talks about the new things that he has learned about himself. He now clearly sees that things hidden for years are affecting him now. He confesses that sex is important for him too: "I just tried to believe it was unimportant." Daphne realizes that she is as much the problem as Murray. "I was available, but underneath quietly unavailable." She understands that she needs to ask whether she really wants the relationship. Murray and Daphne are working together on shifting gears and shaping a new way of being to-

gether. It is too early to know if they are going to make it together, but at least now that basic issues are surfacing, they have
a fighting chance.

FIRST PHASE: DEMASKING

Shifting gears is not as easy as it sounds in our age of automatic transmissions. There is nothing automatic about it. It
seems to be a process of at least three distinguishable phases. In
the first phase, the masks come off. Under the masks lie fear,
anger, and despair. Even though I no longer want to project on
my partner, making him or her the brunt of my anger, fear, or
aloneness, some of it is bound to come out as I wrestle and struggle with my inner ghosts. The demasking is, nevertheless, essential to my growth. My unresolved anger prevents me from giving
myself as I desire in my relationship. My fear of nonacceptance
keeps me at a safe distance. My despair makes me feel that, in
the end, nothing will work anyway.

Paradoxically, it is only when we own our anger, fear, and despair that we are on the way to being free of them. It is precisely
unowned anger and fear that keep us locked up in ourselves.
Not acknowledging the problem cuts us off from a genuine solution. Denying our anger, our dependency, and our loneliness
makes us victims of anger, dependency, and loneliness. Nothing
can be done when we refuse to accept the inner reality. Pretending to be unafraid when we desperately fear abandonment
makes us hostages of the fear. At any time these unresolved fears
and angers can flare up and dictate our behavior. In reaction we
often hold even more tightly to our masks. We seek ever new
ways to keep things in check. We become rigid, uptight, encased
in ways of being that choke our spirit and freeze our heart. Our
muscles tense, our jaw tightens, our shoulders hunch.

Breaking through the body armoring and setting aside the
masks is never easy; it takes courage and support. But when it
happens, whether suddenly or slowly, there are the beginnings
of new growth and life. Owning our fears and angers and facing
our despair allows us to integrate them into our lives in healthy
and constructive ways. Instead of constantly fighting to keep
them down and under control, we work with them directly to

put them in their proper place. We learn that we do not need to be so afraid of our anger or our fear. Despair can turn into hope. But until we have faced our anger, fear, and despair, it is virtually impossible for us to really open our heart and give ourselves freely to another person. When we are consumed by unresolved anger, how can our tender feelings come to expression? They cannot. They may easily come out as violence. An extreme example of this phenomenon is wife beaters and sexual abusers of children. Often we don't even know what it means to be tender and loving. Our emotional tank, so to speak, is overflowing with anger and hate.

This first stage of Shifting Gears can be very hard on each of the partners. Although each of us knows that much of the anger that comes our way is a legacy from early unresolved traumas, we still feel the effects of that anger on us. We may know that a certain reaction is triggered by a deeply ingrained fear that has nothing to do with us; nevertheless we feel it when our partner withdraws and sulks. We know that basic emotional patterns were set in the first six years of our lives. We may even be aware of the unresolved experiences with parents, siblings, other nurturers, or God that largely explain what is going on in our partner. Yet we experience firsthand the hurt and rejection.

In fact, a partner's presence usually serves to intensify the early experience, for often we were first attracted to each other because on an unconscious level we saw possibilities to reenact the original drama with our parents. We made our partner into a new version of our parents in a vain attempt to rectify the earlier misconnection. We treated him or her as a new version of the longed for love object. When we are going through the painful process of dismantling our defenses and acknowledging our deepest unmet needs, our partner is a red flag that immediately and constantly confronts us with our inadequacies and guilts.

In this delicate and painful passage, it is exceedingly helpful if we can reassure our partner that our being out of sorts is basically not because of him or her. "It's the pain of feeling unloved as a child." "It's the fear that there will be nothing left of me." "It's my anger at never being able to connect with my father." Such statements are particularly helpful because our partner has his or her own struggle. Most likely, even though our partner may know with the head that something is going on that is not directly connected with him or her, in the gut he or she is not so sure. Often we use precisely such situations to do our own projections and prove to ourselves how unlovable and undesirable we really are.

SECOND PHASE: DISTANCING

The second phase of Shifting Gears flows out of the demasking. My partner is a constant reminder of my basic traumas. I can't stand it. Distancing of some kind seems necessary. I need to say no before I can in a new way and on a deeper way say yes. This can be an even more excruciating state than Power Struggle. For now, as we untangle our relationship and begin to see each other as the persons we are and not the persons we project, the burning question is whether we will like what we see. The risk is real and scary. That's a basic reason we resist taking off the masks in the first place. What if we don't really like each other?

Distancing occurs in this second phase because I may feel so vulnerable, like a house without a roof, that I cannot be with my partner in that condition. I dearly need my own space; I need to be able to say no to advances. That is especially hard on a spouse who already feels unloved and unwanted and has been struggling with rejection for a lifetime. That spouse will be feeling so vulnerable because he or she is facing the depth of her or his need to be loved and the aching fear that he or she is unlovable. To see a partner being even more distant is anguish.

To know that distancing is a normal part of the process leading to a deeper but not enmeshed connection is exceedingly helpful. My partner is not setting out to reject me. She or he needs to experience her or his own space for a while. Not understanding this has often led to the ruin of a relationship. Feeling the discomfort and distance, the distanced partner can feel utterly rejected and turn elsewhere for solace. In panic or anger he or she gets involved with someone else, often harming the marriage irreparably.

At such junctures it becomes evident whether or not the couple has moved fully into Stage Three. The dovetailing became apparent in Stage Two. The "unloved" spouse desperately wants to pressure the distancing partner to come close. The distancing spouse fights guilt at not giving in to the needy spouse. Genuine advance takes place when both partners can resist their respective temptations to fall into the old ways. Of course there will be relapses. If such patterns were easy to break, they wouldn't be so pernicious, but we are talking about beginnings of change in the dominant pattern.

The partner who needs distance learns to come close not out of guilt, but out of an inner desire to be intimate. If the guilt wins and he or she gives in, that person will likely end up feeling alienated and used once more—the old script. At the same time, the partner who feels the desperate need to be close learns to cease and desist pressuring. For when the pressure is on and the partner responds, that person begins to resent that he or she always has to make the first move and is reconfirmed in the fear that he or she will never be loved freely—the old script.

So, no matter how difficult it is for both parties—and it is lonely as well—both partners need to practice resisting their ingrained impulses. The partners in Stage Three will support each other in this endeavor as much as possible, for they know that giving into their impulses hurts both persons. The individuals are learning to hold on to their own fragile sense of independence. They need to feel justified in being their own persons and in reaching out only when moved to reach out. She learns to handle her fear of abandonment without being immediately rescued. Instead of accusing him of rejecting her and feeling that rejection, she begins to take responsibility for her deepest fear. When such learning takes hold, true intimacy based on mutual sharing and equality is becoming real. When he reaches out, it will be more out of desire to share himself than a movement dictated by guilt. When she reaches out, it will be more out of a desire to give of herself rather than out of an insatiable need to have her emptiness filled.

In the period when some distance seems necessary, times of intimate sharing, including sexual intercourse, may have to be temporarily suspended. We need to get more disentangled from each other before we can find new ways to be together. Saying no to our partner and feeling that this is okay is a necessary prerequisite to saying yes in new and more fulfilling ways.

Here too it is crucial that partners give each other explicit messages. "It's not that I'm rejecting you, but I need time to feel my own space." "I know that I'm sulking because I feel rejected, but I'm struggling with it. And as much as a part of me wants you to give in, I really don't want you to rescue me." Healthy distance during this phase can help keep the partners honest when they do meet.

Once our coming closer or staying away from each other was dictated by our own needs. "I love you" more often than not meant "I need you—right now, in this way." True love flourishes when we are able to see the other person in his or her own right. In true love I seek not to overwhelm you with my person nor to absent myself behind a mask of being there. In true love I give you space to move freely and flourish. And, at the same time, in true love I let your being with all your vitality, feelings, and joys stream into my being. Love is being present for another person and receiving the presence of another person into oneself.

The second phase of distancing ends with the realization that it's okay to be together. Okay may seem to be a very low-key way of putting it, but in fact it underlines something quite dramatic. No longer is our relationship basically part of an old scenario in which we feel burdened because of neediness or guilt or fear. We no longer have to get sucked into our partner's struggle. We can let it be his or her struggle without having to run from it or solve it. It's okay, the relationship is free and open to develop in its own way and with its own style toward the future. The marriage has reached a new level. Growth and change have happened! Instead of demanding that we meet each other's needs, we are now ready to meet in the middle. Instead of a subtle or not so subtle tug-of-war, we are now two people freely sharing themselves in their own rhythm of giving and receiving.

In the security of being grounded from within and in the joy of being together, the pressure is off. The partners grow in sharing more of their deepest selves—their anxieties, their joys and hopes, their sorrows and cares. Each partner is able to pursue his or her various callings, more able to take in the nurture and support of the other. Feeling more secure in themselves and their relationships, partners affirm each other as unique, separate persons with their own way of being in the world with new freedom and vigor. The relationship reaches a more fulfilling level of vibrancy and zest, embracing a surprising serenity and peace. The partners experience increased energy and creativity not only in their marriage, but in all their other relationships, with friends, parents, colleagues, and children.

THIRD PHASE: MEETING IN THE MIDDLE

Without equality, intercourse is a battle for control in which no true intimacy is possible. With equality, sexual intercourse too takes on new depth and meaning as a meeting-in-the-middle. The partners surrender to each other from the heart and become one. Giving up ourselves to each other, we feel an overwhelming sense of oneness and togetherness, touching each other in the depths of our being. And out of the union we receive ourselves back refreshed and affirmed. The old feelings of "needing to be there" or "afraid to be there" begin to dissipate more and more, and when they are present they no longer dominate or paralyze our relating. A sense of "being there" to give and receive as full persons in the mutuality of troth begins to replace the old feelings of guilt and fear. The couple experiences an astounding sense of joy and well-being that often they had considered only a dream.

Stage Three ends with the third phase of partners meeting in the middle.[3] Our deepest intimacy needs are met even as our deepest identity needs are honored. As we discover each other's uniqueness, we yield to each other's needs. The identity-intimacy movement comes into its own. No longer do we use intimacy to make up for a lack of identity, but neither do we fear that intimacy will destroy identity. We need to sense our own identity to really risk a union with another. On the other hand, we need the affirmation of union to move out on our own.

STEVEN AND INGRID

Steven and Ingrid are a shy and sensitive couple who are shifting gears. Like most of us, they need some help. Ingrid came from a family in which her father was the unapproachable authority. When she was an infant, her mother fed her mechanically by the book every four hours. Deep down she feels out of place in her body and fights the horrible feeling that she will never be fully accepted. She has a fear of physical contact but a desperate need for it. Since she got the attention she craved only when she challenged father's authority and he punished her, she became a rebel of sorts. She hated the punishment, but at the same time it was then that she felt most alive. "I want to be close, but I'm afraid that I will be bopped on the head." Through the first years of their marriage, Steven was the safe, nonaggressive, accepting husband who gave her the first home she ever had. But as her deeper needs have slowly surfaced, she sometimes finds him "too good," boring, and unexciting. And she feels guilty, a guilt doubled by the knowledge that Steven is disappointed that they have not had a family.

Steven was the middle son of a German family. Shy and sensitive, he never learned to ask questions and assert himself. And when he did come out with his own thoughts or feelings, they were not liked. His father was a "hard head" who was seldom at home. Steven constantly clashed with mother but usually ended up giving in to her wishes to keep the peace. During his university days, he broke away from home and immigrated to the United States. There he met Ingrid who was looking for a way to escape her situation. She was articulate, able to be vulnerable, and nonthreatening. They soon married. First, it was fine. But gradually he has come to believe that she is really not interested in understanding him. At the same time, just as he couldn't stand up to his mother, he hasn't been able to tell her this.

Both Steven and Ingrid pretended for a long time that things were okay. Neither of them was able to share that their needs were not being met. Instead she would complain about being tired from having to work three days. Steven's answer, "I have to work five days," confirmed for her his lack of support and empathy. Steven became more and more reticent, withdrawing into projects in his new workroom. Every once in a while he would lose patience and say that she wouldn't be so tired if she would exercise more. And he would mention that her tummy was developing a little pot.

Ingrid finally got the courage to ask Steven to come for therapy to help her with her issues. That was the excuse she used. Afterward she was able to admit that she had wanted Steven to hear in therapy that he wasn't meeting her needs. At first he resisted, wary of yet another way in which she could manipulate him. The reason for his wariness came out only after a few sessions. Initially, he didn't think therapy was necessary, but if she really wanted him to come, he would do it—once.

With some encouragement Ingrid was able to express her concern about the lack of zest in their love life. She wanted massage more often, but massage when Steven was really into it. He initially agreed, but suddenly he broke his reticence by retorting, "But you don't put yourself into it when you do it to me. I have my needs too. And they are not being met." Suddenly, Steven and Ingrid were being real with each other. She was relieved that Steven wasn't as satisfied as he often appeared to be. Feeling heard and not put down for saying what he really felt, he began to tell his story. He acknowledged his fear of feelings and difficulty with being vulnerable. Ingrid too has been looking at her own issues in depth. She realizes the truth of some things she didn't want to face about herself. "I've begun to hear the inner 'truth voice' that says, 'yes, it is true!' "

Steven and Ingrid are now in the process of shifting gears. They are scared, but they are realizing that it is even more scary to continue to pretend that things are not too bad when they are in fact mediocre at best. The new zest and spring in their steps, Steven's delight in telling his story, and Ingrid's relief in being able to talk about her deepest needs are good signals of a basic shift in their relationship.

It is in Stage Three of the marriage journey that the back-and-forth movement between identity and intimacy comes into its own in a healthy, balanced fashion. Stage Three does not mean perfection, but it does mean that our relationship, whatever its remaining problems, tensions, and scars, reaches the place where we experience it as fundamentally affirming and deeply satisfying. We have moved through and beyond the competitiveness of the power struggle to the mutuality of partnership. Our relationship has risen above the mediocrity of a settle-for-less arrangement that blunts our spirits and emerges as a fulfilling communion refreshing our spirits. With a heightened sense of our own individuality, we are able to reach out for intimate connection more out of strength than weakness. Meeting in the middle we begin to shape a mutually affirming and fulfilling way of being together that accepts and works with the persons we are. The intimacy of our relationship is more and more grounded in the realism of accepting each other as the persons we are with our gifts and imperfections rather than on the unreality of ethereal illusions. Letting go of our need to change our partner, we shift gears on the way to the mutuality of Stage Four.

6. Stage Four: Mutuality

An encounter
   is a strange
      and wonderful thing
presence
one person to another
present
one to another
   life flowing
      one to another
but
we can be together
   and not meet

we can live in the same house day after day
   sit at the same table
   kneel at the same pew
   read the same books
   but never meet

we can kiss
   gestures of love
   apparent tenderness
      but never meet

a meeting is a strange and wonderful thing

presence one person to another
   present one to another
   life flowing one to another

—JEAN VANIER

Meeting in the middle is a strange and wonderful sharing of a mystery, the mystery each of us is as a gift of God. With open hearts, we reach out and touch each other. As we are encouraged to become more fully who we are, our hearts flutter. Every fiber of our bodies begins to tingle as life flows one to another. In inner connection we experience vital affirmation of ourselves. In being one we remain two. We come near and do not feel devoured. We are intimate and do not take flight. No longer imprisoned by the fear of closeness, we are free to be close. No longer bound by fear, we are able to bond in love. Perfect love casts out fear. Com-passion, com-promise: the mutuality of committed troth.

TRANSITION

We cross the threshold of Stage Four when mutuality-in-troth becomes the main pattern of our relationship. When troth becomes more ease than dis-ease, when love puts fear in its shadow, then we have entered Stage Four. There is an at-one-ment: a belonging without possessiveness, a caring without abusing, a forgiving without blaming.

The mutuality of Stage Four comes rather unexpectedly. Although brewing for a long while, although tasted in earlier stages, when mutuality becomes the fundamental way we are together, it comes like a surprise, overtakes us almost unawares. Yet its reality is unmistakable and undeniable.

We felt that something monumental was changing in Stage Three, but the joy of the new way of being was often cancelled when the old ghosts and the old fears reemerged. In times of stress we still too often held back in panic or lashed out in defiance. The risk of love was still too great. The fear that we might lose what we had going between us often triggered the old patterns of enmeshment and alienation. Stage Three gave us encouraging glimpses of a new way of being, only to be followed by the same old disappointing and paralyzing reenactments of the past. At times, we could not help wondering if we would ever get off the roller coaster.

Then it happens—just when we are wondering if we can ever get out of the old ruts. With all the scars and scares, we discover that we are living a new reality together! Looking back, we can trace the signs of transformation; nevertheless, we are surprised by joy when it happens. It feels so unexpected and undeserved that we hesitate to acknowledge the new stage of being in words. Words may chase it away. Anyway, how can words capture this ineffable delight of two lovers in communion, the healing mystery?!

But eventually the good news cannot be repressed. New life will cry out. In looks and actions, buoyed up by good feelings and tender caresses, the emerging intimacy takes shape. Words are spoken and heard in new ways. No longer instruments of defense and attack, words become bearers of truth and grace. Dagger words are replaced by bonding words of caring and sharing. With belonging and connection instead of alienation and disconnection, the relationship has entered a deeper stage of mutuality. None of this need be momentous, but for the partners it is rare and precious in its quiet ordinariness. Everything is the same, yet everything is different.

I remember vividly the moment I looked at pictures taken on my twenty-fifth wedding anniversary. Like a spectator peering at someone else, I noticed that the man looked happy and that the couple looked happy together. Then I realized: "That is me. And yes, I am happy. What shows on the outside is what I am feeling on the inside." Until that moment I had not dared to put it into words. Even as I write it now, I cannot do so without a surge of feeling, of joy, but also of sadness that it took so long.

OPEN FACES, OPEN HEARTS

In Stage Three we changed our perceptions of ourselves and of our relationship. As individuals we owned our shadow sides, stopped projecting on each other, and repented. Turning away from games, blame, and paranoia, we experienced in our relationship a change of heart. We gave up the pretenses that armored us against intimacy. As we accepted our rage, fear, resentment, and despair, our will to power, our devils and demons, in the paradox of grace we experienced a new freedom to be ourselves. The foundations of our individual identities were reformed and, at the same time, the foundations of our communal identity were being transformed. The Scriptures speak of the need of *metanoia*, change of heart. *Metanoia*, repentance on the part of self, leads to forgiveness of the other. In Stage Three and Stage Four our change of heart begins to show itself in a change in our way of relating.

The structure of our way of being together is fundamentally altered: compassion replaces alienation, letting be replaces needing to control. Stage Four marks a new stage of growth in intimacy on the foundations of troth. It does not mean that we have arrived or even that we have in our hands a formula for success. The relationship is not perfect. We come to accept that not every part of our selves is nourished in this one intimacy, but we do experience an inner connection that enlarges the heart and gladdens the spirit.

It does mean that we are at a new stage in our journey. Forgiveness forges another way. We are released from our prisons of blame and projection. Disillusioned with our old ways, we can busy ourselves with forming better ways. Owning our own brokenness, we no longer need to hide it from each other. In open conversation with ourselves we can converse freely with each other. Free to be ourselves, we are freed to see our partner as the unique person he or she is. No longer needing to defend ourselves at every turn, we are able to take in the reality of the other person as ally instead of invader. Accepting the self I am, I can accept you without demands. Thus, we are empowered to deepen intimacy.

Without many of the hidden cords that keep us entangled, we are able to give more freely to each other. I want you free, open-faced and open-hearted. Your freedom is my gain, for then I need not fear entrapment and abuse. I can trust that you are reaching out to me for me. You do not want to master me. You desire to delight in my presence. And your openness of spirit calls forth a free response from my center. So we become initiators and sponsors of each other's freedom. Liberty is the song of love. "For freedom Christ has set us free" (Gal. 5:1). Bonded heart to heart, we are free.

The giving of two selves becomes a rhythm of forgiving in the present, forgetting the past, and foretasting the future. Meeting in the middle, we are able to celebrate our mutual troth. A positive troth cycle develops that slowly but surely deepens our intimacy and quells our desperation. We become more liberated to be near—without fear of engulfment. We become more free to be apart—without fear of devastation. I am able to let my partner in on who I am and where I am—without fear of rejection. And my partner is able to be there without having to stay aloof or rescue—without the pain of guilt. Neither of us needs to get sucked into the struggle of the other, but at the same time, we are able to let ourselves be important to each other and allow ourselves to ask something of each other. We are able to express and own our basic needs and we feel secure to be with each other in spite of these needs. My partner's need no longer holds me captive or scares me away. We are separate and inter-dependent rather than dependent and enmeshed. When we are able to be open in each other's presence without the urge to flee or the desire to possess, then intimacy has become ours.

HORACE AND PAMELA

Horace and Pamela asked for help even before they got married. They loved each other but aware of their own patterns and, having gone through previous relationships, they were very aware of areas that needed work. Under pressure Horace floats into a dream world, is not present, and infuriates Pamela. Horace needs to resist the pressure of her anger and have his own space, but he feels guilty when he does. At the same time, he is furious that Pamela wants him around constantly. Then he just wants to run. In fact, one of his big fears is that he will just pick up and leave one day. Pamela in turn finds herself continually hounding him and then feeling guilty about it.

During the last years the relationship turned a new corner when they began to understand that Pamela's fury erupts not (as they both thought) because she needs to control his every move, but because she is looking for constant assurance that he will not leave her. Since happiness entered her life with Horace, she is very sensitive to any hint of abandonment. Being able to name Pamela's basic concern relieved the tension that was beginning to fray the relationship. Horace began to be able to do his own thing without guilt and Pamela has been able to let go some of her need for constant reassurance. As a result Horace enjoys being with her more, doesn't as often retreat into his dreamy state, and Pamela feels Horace's genuine affection and doesn't feel as resentful of Horace's own projects. Horace is working on his fear that he can never give himself completely. Pamela is working on her need for Horace to give her life. Horace has learned to look Pamela in the eye. He is not as afraid; she is not as anxious. Committed to each other, the two of them have shifted gears. They have taken off masks, have given each other more space, enjoy times of meeting in the middle, and are beginning to experience the stability and vulnerability of Stage Four.

VULNERABLE, YET SECURE

Intimacy is vulnerability. But intimacy in troth is also security; it means I am at home, safe, and sheltered. Exposing myself, being open and vulnerable is most scary, but when in my vulnerability I feel received and accepted, what deep joy! That's the troth paradox: we feel vulnerable, yet secure; fully exposed, defenseless, and naked, yet clothed. When I discover and accept your boundaries, and you mine, we can be ourselves, unafraid in each other's presence.

Meeting in the middle is nonthreatening, for we are no longer attempting to force a liaison on our own terms. Mutuality rather than mastery is the goal. In the middle, on common ground, we give ourselves willingly and freely to each other: voluntary surrender, letting be and letting go, merging and joining. When we separate, as we inevitably do, our identity returns reaffirmed and enlarged. Instead of morning-after bitterness or resentment, we can experience the release of incredible energy for more giving and receiving.

The more intimate we are, the more we need and receive the respect and honor that is our due as holy image-bearers of God. My responsibility to you is to honor your uniqueness as a gift and to hear the mystery of your call. The more we reveal to each other, the less there is to hide and the more secure we can feel. I love you: I sense your innermost vulnerability and I honor your tender boundaries. Fear not! And I reach out from my center to be with you, affirming and caring. Being there from the center is the kind of presence that always makes a difference.

Together we learn to know and respect the boundaries of
our intimacy.

INTIMACY WITHOUT FEAR

Touched by mutual presence and unconditional affirmation,
two hearts pulse together. Joy flows through our senses. It is
good that you exist and that I exist—together, committed. Words
fail when speaking about joy. Often words come more easily
when we share pain, suffering, and tragedy; somehow they seem
more true to the human scene. Nevertheless, joy is an essential
ingredient of intimacy. Without joy—not manufactured sensation or frantic scurrying, but the contentment that surprises—
there is no time or place for the amazed lingering that is the
heart and mystery of intimacy. Without joy, we remain empty
and ravished, nervous lest we miss out on something, obsessed
and on the run.

Fear freezes; joy thaws. Sluggish hearts begin to stream with
the waters of love. As every fiber of our bodily existence vibrates
with energy, we can taste and see that life is good. The arrival
of joy is a sign of the Spirit's healing presence (Rom. 14:17). We
can be together, and it's good. It is not always (or even mainly)
high-intensity baring of the soul. It may be as simple (and as
difficult!) as the mutual enjoyment of a cup of tea or a walk in
the woods. Joy is intimacy without fear.

Inner joy is connection within myself. Marital joy is intimate
connection with my partner. Connection gives us a sense of well-
being, a reason to be, a surge of power, a flow of hope, a rush
of joy. To be reconnected with God, self, others, and the world
is the joy of redemption. Joy calls us to live together more fully
and deeply in the Presence for the healing of ourselves, other
persons, and all of God's creatures. It means taking more risks,
deepening our intimacy, and strengthening our bond of troth.
It means plumbing the depths of our relationship, taking our
sexuality into hitherto unexplored heights of intimacy, ventilat-
ing our angers and fears in more healthy ways, growing in sensitivity to the strengths and weaknesses of each other, developing

fresh modes of expressing our delight in each other's presence. Commitment to each other and to the God who nourishes us pulls and stretches us even further than we dared imagine.

MUTUALITY

Stage Four means mutual commitment. It means mutual availability, a promise of our presence with and for each other. Mutuality is for equals. Mutuality means two-way openness without games and masks. Mutuality speaks of kinship of spirit, sincerity of heart, reciprocity of soul, compatibility of body. Mutuality is the flowering of the tender plant of troth.

Troth is sharing each other without fear or insecurity. Troth is caring without strings. It is gentle hands that know when to touch and when to hold back. Troth takes time; its spontaneity evolves slowly. Troth cannot be forced. Troth is patient, honest, and forgiving. Troth is fragile and durable, tender and strong, playful and serious, spontaneous and predictable. Too much water or too little water, too much light or too little light brings blight or death. Troth develops in the humus of commonality rather than in the sterile soil of conformity. Partners in troth grow together, give each other space, and are noncompetitive. They do not automatically share everything with each other, but they share each other.

The mutuality of troth is a delicate, finely tuned relationship, rich with paradox and promise. Two people, secure in their own identities, bask in each other's acceptance. Two people choose, not out of need or fear, to edge out on the dangerous limb of troth slowly together. First one and then the other takes the lead, depending on time, situation, and talents.

LISA AND PAUL

Lisa and Paul had a perfectly dovetailed relationship, safe but ultimately dangerous. Paul is an articulate, intellectual blue blood from Montreal and Lisa is an intense, dark-haired beauty from Spain. They came to therapy because the truce in their twelve-year marriage was breaking. Paul was depressed and listless; Lisa was tense and very guarded. He is a very successful professional who has felt like a total fiasco at home. Lisa has stayed home to take care of their five children and has put a lot of energy into community and church work.

Lisa complained that Paul was no longer trustworthy, didn't give himself, constantly forgot, and always did the wrong thing at home. Paul was so desperate to please that he meekly agreed that he was guilty on all points. He was so afraid of crossing her that he was unaware of his own rage. He just kept saying, "I love you"—with the unspoken trailer, "Why don't you love me?" Lisa was Paul's feeling regulator. When she sobbed, he would start crying. (Then she would suddenly stop.) She was his queen who could do no wrong, the ideal warm, loving mother he never had who would rescue him from his isolation. He lived by the illusion, "Maybe today, if I'm a good boy, I will be loved."

It became apparent that underneath her bold front Lisa was as fragile as Paul. She was the anxious little girl who needed Paul to be perfect in order for her to relax. He had to be the secure, reliable father she never had. She lived by the illusion, "If I don't grow up, one day I will be loved by Father." Her mother had fed that very illusion by drumming into her that she wasn't old enough to do what she wanted. On the surface, he was the taker and she the giver. On a deeper level, he was "victim" who was always giving, she was "persecutor" who was always harping away and punishing. He pleased so he would get. She blamed to avoid having to give what she feared she didn't have. He covered his anger by feeling sorry for himself and by being depressed. She hid her guilt by putting him down and being sure that he is only out to use her. Paul's willingness to do anything was keeping Lisa the little girl. Lisa's withholding of herself and of sexual contact when she was displeased kept Paul a little boy. Lisa felt hopeless. Paul felt rejected. Both felt empty inside.

In therapy over a period of years Paul has learned to gain a firmer sense of himself and stand his ground. He has been able to own his anger. He no longer thinks that he is automatically wrong. He is less panicky inside, more caring, and lives less in his head. Lisa's growth and change has been more gradual and subtle. She grew in understanding that she was recreating her own family history in which her badgering mother drove her father away. For a while she closed down in despair, unable to respond to Paul. But now she is slowly learning to stop projecting on Paul, to let down and give up her need for control, and she is not as paralyzed by her inner despair. She is beginning to take full responsibility for her own life as a woman. By looking at their own character structures and admitting their games, Lisa and Paul are developing a new acceptance of each other and slowly extricating themselves from their entanglement. Their journey has not been easy, but they have shifted gears and are moving into the mutuality of Stage Four. They are beginning to learn to give each other the space of love and to trust that the times of flowing together will happen in the dance of intimacy. Through all the steps and missteps of their dance, their commitment to God and to each other has been a tremendous source of strength for both of them.

SEXUALITY

In the mutuality of Stage Four sexuality deepens and is integrated with love. Sexuality, the mysterious reciprocal attraction that people experience together, is woven into the whole character of who we are as persons. Our sexuality urges us toward a deep and personal relationship, most often to a union of committed love.

In our society, eros or the primal urge to connect is often reduced to physical, genital sex. But severing our physical sexuality from the totality of who we are makes us into victims of its power. It becomes demonic even as we try to make it divine. Sexuality becomes an instrument for evil

—when the urge to share becomes the urge to dominate
—when we live by the illusion that genital sex can by itself create instant communion
—when despair results in promiscuity
—when we withdraw into asexuality
—when sexuality is a way to escape
—when sexuality is glamorized as the be-all and end-all of life.

When our emotional life is healthy, we adjust to our sexual feelings without being dominated by them or by repressing them. Fully accepting our sexuality, including our physical drive and erotic feelings, we integrate them into our total acting and loving. This integrative process is determined almost completely by the way all our other emotions have evolved and were integrated prior to puberty.

In adult intimate relations we have opportunities to resolve, integrate, and deepen sexual feelings and expressions in the same way that we work through other unresolved feelings from childhood. The very same problems affecting our relationship as a whole will arise with particular intensity in our sexual relations. Without equality and mutuality sexual intercourse becomes a battle for control in which no intimacy is really possible. We come on strong to defend against intimacy, to vent pent-up anger, or to ward off desperation. We employ sex to reward, manipulate, and punish, as a carrot to dangle and pull back. We use sex to bolster weak egos and to reassure ourselves that we are alive.

In our culture the mutual enjoyment of sex is often frustrated by differing patterns of sexual response in many men and women. For many modern males emotional closeness is closely identified with or submerged in sexual closeness. When feelings are sexualized in this way, sex easily becomes the main route to deep and tender feelings. For most women, on the other hand, emotional closeness is a prerequisite to full sexual enjoyment. Ann Landers recently reported that seventy-two percent of more than ninety thousand women said that they actually preferred cuddling to sex. Landers said that she was especially surprised by the fact that of the seventy-two percent, forty percent were under age forty. In this common pattern, sex is a problem: men needing sex before they can let down and feel close, women needing to feel close before they can fully give themselves to sex.

For both sexes intercourse has in many instances become a joyless coupling in which, as in *Annie Hall*, the inner self is a detached observer sitting on a chair. Partners seem to go along, but they may lose the ability to respond sexually, becoming impotent or frigid. It is not only the submissive partner who is afraid of being overwhelmed. The very need to dominate is a defense against giving up control and being vulnerable.

There are at least four different ways in which we can experience sexual intercourse. When intercourse is basically physical release and essentially self-gratification, we have physical sex. When intercourse especially affirms us emotionally, providing feelings of closeness and reassurance, we have connection sex. When intercourse is an expression of giving and sharing of self, we have self-expressive sex. When intercourse is the unitive celebration of the mutual commitment and inner connection of two lovers, we have commitment sex. Commitment sex celebrates our heart-to-heart bonding and is dependent on it. With such betrothed connection, sex can be an ecstatic experience of the promise: "And the two shall be one flesh."

As part of the highest stage of love, commitment sex includes the other ways. We give of ourselves, are affirmed personally, and experience physical fulfillment. Self-expressive sex often includes affirmation and release. And connection sex generally mingles with the sexual release. Commitment sex is the sex for which we yearn, but in the ups and downs of human relations the other kinds of intercourse can become dominant or completely separate modes. And there will even be times in commitment sex that the physical heights or emotional connection is not very intense or not very fulfilling. At times, to perhaps give another nuance to an old saying, the spirit is willing, but the flesh is weak.

We fool ourselves if we think that sex in marriage always reaches the commitment level. Sometimes we have sex more out of physical urgings or emotional need than out of a desire to share ourselves and celebrate our union. There is nothing wrong or unusual about that, but it is good to acknowledge it. When our bodies speak more "I need" than "I love" during sex, to say "I love you" is apt to confuse our partner because it clashes with his or her experience.

In the mutuality of Stage Four, our sexual relations, like the rest of our relating, acquire a new depth of honesty and a new height of satisfaction. The sex act becomes a most powerful enactment of mutuality: approach, entrance/reception, full union, withdrawal. Two equal and separate identities become one flesh, giving themselves up and regaining themselves. Abandoning ourselves in mutual union we receive ourselves back expanded and deepened. For a joyous moment we pass beyond fear, lower our barriers, open our hearts, meet, touch, join, and are fulfilled.

In the intoxication of Romance, intercourse is a delight of sensation and passion, but when our differences emerge in Stage Two, intercourse becomes a powerful tool for intimidation and control. Protestations of love often cover over the reality of what is happening. All our unresolved issues crowd in. Some couples keep these issues in abeyance by, in fact, making intercourse basically an act of physical gratification. However, the vulnerability of heart and soul that is natural to intercourse makes it increasingly impossible for most couples to isolate their sex life from the ongoing emotional dynamics of the marriage. Intercourse becomes a strained and tense jockeying back and forth, often hurtful and desperate, an accurate barometer of the relationship as a whole.

A telling sign of a shift from the power struggle of Stage Two is less pressured and more satisfying sex. It is okay to be together without having to do our controlling or submitting number on each other. As part of the ongoing shift, we discover an ability to reconcile our sexual differences: We learn to reach out and engage in sex more because we want to give and share of ourselves and less because we need to appease or dominate to get our needs met. We discover the difference between sex as intimacy rising from a desire to share self and sex as maneuvers we engage in because we need to or are expected to. We learn to make sex a way of being-together rather than of doing-to-each-other. In Stage Four the enjoyment of our sexuality beyond fear becomes our lived experience. Doing-to becomes unnecessary; being-with is deep joy. The letting-be together—the miracle of oneness which always takes our breath away!—is a mark of true love.

The being-with of Stage Four naturally takes on many shapes and forms, like a meandering river, depending on inclination, time, and situation. Anything that is done together may become infused with a peace that passes understanding. Washing dishes together can become a sacrament of intimacy. In the same way, a couple can enjoy a total bodily streaming together. It is from the quiet quivering of such pleasure that partners on occasion merge and let go in the rhythms of intercourse. Or edging our bodies together like nesting spoons, we touch, purr, and commune.

I MESSAGES

Open and honest communication is also a mark of mutuality. We say what we mean and we mean what we say. That is more difficult than we often think. In my case, I'm not always sure what I mean. I often know what I am expected to say, and that's a temptation because the approval I want so much can be mine. I often know what nasty things I want to say, and that's hard to resist because it offers me a ready outlet for frustration. Or I know what I should say—but I don't because it means owning up to a shortcoming or admitting my ignorance. And sometimes the turmoil within leaves me so genuinely at sea that I batten down the hatches and talk and talk. But I don't know what I mean or don't mean because I am out of touch with my inner self.

Words from the heart reach out and connect people, but often we use words to distort reality, disconnecting and misleading people. Sentences can be fences behind which we hide, defenses that make it impossible for anyone to reach us. Often we insist on the truth of what we have said even when our body gives another message. We speak words of joy when it is clear that we are utterly depressed. Beet red, eyes blazing, we deny that we are upset. In fact, for most of us, nonverbal body language speaks more loudly and clearly than our words.

A perfectly ordinary sentence like "Boy, do I want to thank you for the telephone call last week" said in a certain context with a special tone and emphasis can mean "Your call was a life saver. I thought no one cared." Or it can mean, "You bastard, why didn't you have the courtesy to return my call?" Words can nourish or words can stab; they can encourage or they can provoke.

In the struggle of intimacy, words become effective weapons. We use them to dig at our partner ("You always . . . ," "You never . . ."), to point the finger ("How many times do I have to tell you . . . ," "You know how much that upsets me, yet . . ."), and to deny ("That's just not true . . . ," "There you go again, blaming . . ."). I always knew when my mother was displeased with me; she would say "James" rather than "Jim." To this day, I feel like a bad boy when someone calls me James.

We especially use words for camouflage, for disguising our guilt, hiding vulnerability, keeping things on the surface. As a marriage counselor I have learned to recognize that a sure sign of serious trouble is two totally different accounts of the same event. One can with a high degree of accuracy predict the level of trouble by looking at the degree of similarity and difference in the two stories. I still recall my amazement when as a beginning therapist I was listening to one married couple. The woman was complaining that her husband never wanted to do anything together. I asked for an example. "Well," she said, "last winter we went for a weekend to a cottage in snow country. The next morning I asked my husband if he would like to go skiing. He said no." I turned to the husband. "She never asked me," he said. I was nonplussed.

I persisted; I said to her, "What precisely did you say?" She told me that she had looked outdoors at the newly fallen snow and said, "Today looks like a good time to be outdoors." "Is that all?" I groaned. Before she could reply, her husband spoke up. "Now I remember. That's exactly what she said. I think that she even glanced at the skis standing by the door. But that morning I felt like doing my water colors, and that's what I did. She never asked me to ski. But I guess that I knew all along what she really wanted." Suddenly, it all became clear. She was afraid that he would reject her offer, so she chose the indirect method. In that way she could avoid having to face a direct no from him. And the husband played along. Not wanting to cause a scene by saying no, he conveniently ignored her and went about his business.

With practice this couple learned to communicate more directly and more meaningfully. She discovered that a no from her husband in response to a particular question was not to be taken as a total rejection of herself as a person. Her fear that this was the case had led her to never really ask directly. The husband admitted that he resented her constant, unspoken accusations, and even though he felt guilty, he found himself pushing her away.

At about the same time I discovered that I played similar word games. Instead of saying, "I would like to go to a movie tonight. Are you interested in coming along?" I would say, "Would you like to go to the movie?" I was wearing my "pleasing" mask and the thought never entered my mind that I was putting my wife on the spot. But she knew that I would be sorely disappointed at a no. In fact, I regularly sulked. My being "nice" was giving her sole responsibility for decisions. Her resentment began to grow and I picked it up as rejection. So whether we went to the movie or stayed home, we seldom had a wonderful time.

There are four types of messages we use when we communicate with our partners.[1] There are topic messages such as "the gas tank is empty" or "it's a sunny day." For many of us these third-person, out-there kind of comments make up the bulk of our conversation with each other. There are partner messages such as "you forgot to fill up the gas tank" or "do you want to go skiing?" Partner messages are the perfect vehicle for blaming and putting the responsibility on the other person. There are I messages such as "I need gas" or "I would like to go skiing." I messages are personal but risky. That's why many of us prefer topic and partner messages. But they are also the kind of messages that make for intimacy. Finally, there are relationship messages such as "I noticed that the tank is still empty. Didn't you find a station open?" or "I'm into skiing, are you?" These messages are the stuff of intimacy. We say where we are and we reach out to the other.

I messages and relationship messages help keep things straight and clean. Saying "I was hurt by your comment" is an admission of vulnerability and a request for an explanation. Saying "you hurt me when you said that" is assignment of blame that freezes the situation. The partner can either deny it, admit guilt, or beat around the bush. In any case the temperature is not suitable for the growth of intimacy. Topic messages are just as inhospitable to intimacy—often more so because they leave the other person guessing. Does "the gas tank is empty" mean I am being accused of not doing my job? Is it a request or an order that I fill the tank? Maybe it's telling me that I have been using the car too much. Or is it wondering out loud where I went yesterday afternoon? Or is it an attempt to make up by saying "I will fill the tank"?

Parents also easily hide behind partner messages in putting their children down. I heard of a mother recently who yelled at her teenager, "How can you study with that music blaring. Shut it off." The teenager retorted, "Doesn't bother me." Mother was stymied. Daughter was upset. End of conversation. In discussion it became clear that the mother really wanted to say, "I don't like that music." Whereupon the daughter replied, "Why didn't you say that?" They then began a good discussion in which the mother explained that she worried about the influence of such music and thought the lyrics were particularly degrading to women. The daughter said that what she liked was the beat, and it allowed her to concentrate on her studies. Stating clearly what we really mean opens the way to understanding and deepened intimacy.

Communication experts tell us that by far the greatest percentage of our messages are of the topic or partner kind. There is an excellent exercise couples can do to become more aware of their communication patterns. Each partner begins with two blank sheets of paper. They divide one paper into four squares—topic, partner, I, relationship—the size of each square to be determined by the percentage of their own communications they estimate fall into each category. Then on the second sheet, they work out what they believe to be their partner's pattern. In each square the partners fill in sample messages they say and hear all the time. Then the partners exchange sheets and discuss them. Most often the paucity of intimacy fostering sentences becomes painfully clear. So does the fact that we tend to overestimate the percentage of intimacy statements we make and underestimate the percentage made by our partner.

It is in Stage Three that couples learn to speak more consistently in "I" and "relationship" ways. And it is in Stage Four that it becomes a settled and easy pattern, a clear sign of the mutuality that is theirs. At any stage it is extremely helpful for couples to practice using "I" sentences. I still taste the relief of saying "I would like to go to the movie. Are you interested in coming along?" I no longer take a no as personal rejection. So whether there is a yes and we go, or a no and I go alone (or with a friend), we feel good. In the paradox of intimacy, when partners feel that their feelings and desires have been acknowledged, they may change their minds. "I don't want to go. But I sense that you want to go very much, so let's go." When we experience that our uniqueness is honored, we are freed to reach out and yield to our partner's wishes.

EXPRESSING FEELINGS

From the book *Talking Together* comes another most helpful exercise for couples.[2] The partners are given a long list of feelings and are asked to put a check mark under the appropriate columns: do they experience this feeling "most of the time," "often," "frequently," "once in a while," or "seldom"? Then the partners go over the list of feelings and check off how often they express in words their particular feeling to their partner. Often an amazing gap appears between frequency of feeling and frequency of expression. I may feel "sexy" quite often, but rarely put it into words. I may always be "bored," but never admit to it. Finally, the partners exchange sheets, requesting a response to their self-perceptions. Usually the exercise deepens the intimacy. Often partners are told, "I can tell when you feel that way, even when you don't say it," or "I would never have guessed that you felt that way," or the surprise of, "I thought you knew how I felt and were deliberately rubbing it in," or, "when you act that way I think that you're feeling angry. What a relief to know that you're feeling embarrassed. Why didn't you tell me before?"

FRANK AND ANDREA

Andrea and Frank are a couple we met in Chapter 2. Since Frank does a lot of walking on the job, he tends to sit down on every possible occasion when he is out with Andrea. They can be shopping together when suddenly Frank will disappear. He has found a chair somewhere. Or they are at the zoo looking at the pandas and suddenly Frank is sitting on a bench. Andrea is disconcerted when he fades away and immediately concludes that he is bored. But afraid to ask him directly, she goes over and says "What's the matter with you?" Upset that she is checking up on him again, he mutters a bit but says no more. She concludes that he is bored; he is perturbed that she can't let him be alone for a moment.

What a moment of relief for both when he was able to say, "When I feel tired, I need to sit down. It doesn't at all mean that I am bored." Frank is learning to say how he feels and he is letting Andrea know when he wants to sit. No doubt he will be bored sometimes, and it will be hard to say so. But his saying how he feels is particularly helpful for Andrea who is afraid that Frank doesn't want to be with her and, when he is silent, feels like she is dragging him along like a child. When he states his position, she can't so easily withdraw into her negativity. It is paying increasing dividends to Frank too, because when he used to go and sit down without saying anything, underneath he admitted to tinges of guilt, as if he were running away from his mother. And when she came and "checked up," he did in fact feel resentful. When nothing was said, Andrea often came home feeling disconnected but angry at herself for wanting to scold Frank. And sensing Andrea's disapproval, Frank would feel bewildered and still a bit guilty. He thought they'd had a good time together. What had he done wrong this time?

EMOTIONAL CLEARANCE

Feelings are gifts we give and need to give if we are to be intimate. Withholding because we don't want to hurt our partner is most likely a cover-up for our fear of making ourselves vulnerable. Covering up does hurt our partner, for then we are not sharing ourselves. On the other hand, dumping on the other person can also be a defense against our own deepest feelings of inadequacy. We all have our own patterns that we need to own and deal with if we are to be honest in our gift giving.

When I give my feelings to you, I am giving of myself, but that does not mean that I am merely my emotions. That is simply not true. We are much more than our angers and fears, our joys and sorrows. We are selves designed by God for love with many capacities and many gifts. The point is that unless I share the feelings of love that stir in my heart, you are unable to judge the genuineness and depth of my love. Love without feeling is thin and suspect.

Feeling acknowledgement and feeling clearance is a large part of mutual intimacy. Being able to express how we feel without causing the other to feel guilty and being able to hear where the other person is without feeling guilty ourselves clears the paths for intimacy. Emotional clearance clears the way for good intellectual discussion. For unless we feel emotionally connected, differences of opinion are difficult to tolerate and often very threatening. Some of us need to learn to share even though we know that we may be misunderstood by our partner. Others of us need to unlearn our tendency to be "good little boys and girls" who are always super nice and never react with anger even when people dump on us. Since every emotional response is a self-revelation, all of us need to develop an acute sensitivity to our emotional patterns of response. We need to ask ourselves: Why did I fly into anger? Where did my fear come from? What caused me to lose my bearings? Why is my first response always no?

I needed to unlearn my tendency to withdraw when I feel I have nothing to contribute or when I can't rescue the situation. According to my learned script, acceptance comes through approval for taking responsibility and being able to handle things. If I can't do that I feel inadequate, unworthy, unloved, and—the bottom line—unlovable. I fall into depression. It is as if there is a curtain of glass cutting me off from others. I see and observe what is happening from a distance, but I am powerless to slide the curtain aside and come out. I long for someone to break through the glass and pull me out.

I am learning to acknowledge when I feel lousy and to realize that I need not withdraw if things don't work out just the way I want. It was a big step to admit I needed help because my script told me I needed to be strong. If being strong didn't give me enough love, certainly admitting weakness would give even less. I had to face the despair underneath it all: the conviction that I was unlovable.

In therapy I was helped to face some of my deepest fears. And I learned to acknowledge that I had looked to my partner to convince me that I was lovable. But since I didn't really believe it myself, my reaching out to her had a desperate quality about it ("give me life!"). When partners begin to face their deepest traumas, they can learn to stop projecting on each other. Up to that point, their very lives depend on avoiding the truth about themselves. In that situation, mutuality is impossible. Deep fears, dovetailing, and the illusions in which we hide from life: those are the truths that must be faced before we can be free.

DOLDRUMS AND SQUALLS

Two people who have achieved Stage Four together have a mutual treasure that is most precious. They know what a gift they have. As they carefully tend it, nurturing each other, they grow from troth to troth. The marriage is moving along full sail.

But even at Stage Four we are still the same people, even though we have changed in many ways. Under stress we may fall into the old traps, hear the old voices, and reenact the old scripts. Perhaps it is our work schedule or a disappointment in another relationship, concern that our children have openings to fulfilling careers or maybe a sickness, whatever—some event triggers the old fears. The old fears of desperation and abandonment, the familiar feelings of guilt and inadequacy are suddenly there, full-blown. Hostilities break out or depression sets in.

Has nothing really changed? Once again we are out of step with each other. We imagine that we are starting over, just when we thought the heavy weather was finally over for good. We were just settling down into a mutually satisfying way of being together. Then we hit a flat spot and we are thrown for a loop. Before, it would have taken more than a flat spot to unnerve us. But now our defenses are down. We didn't expect it. We are stopped short. Maybe we have been fooling ourselves about where we are. We begin to get on each other's nerves, not that anyone else would know. But the partners both know that this spell of quiet is more a fear of relapse than a communion that needs no words.

But after a day or two, maybe a week, one or both of the two partners dares to give voice to the uneasy calm. "I sense something must be bugging you. Anyway when I can't seem to find you, I begin to feel lonely again." "I've been into some old stuff again. Someone I met triggered old fears. I just want you to know that it's not you." "I didn't realize it, but now I know that underneath I was quite anxious about the folks coming." And, suddenly, as quickly as the break, the connection is made. A breeze begins to stir. The stillness is broken.

The marriage has just come through a case of the doldrums. During a doldrums time, nothing is basically amiss in the relationship, but outside forces take it hostage for a spell. In Stage Two we appreciated lulls in the storm. They gave us some hope that things might be getting better. We soon learned that the storm in all its fury was yet to be unleashed. But this is not a lull in the dis-ease that marks Stage Two. No, this is a Stage Four doldrums, a patch of un-ease breaking a stretch of ease. Doldrums are times without wind, and nothing can be done about them. In any marriage, even the best, they happen. They simply have to be endured in the hope and with the knowledge that the wind will pick up.

A sure sign that a couple is in the doldrums of Stage Four and not the lulls of Stage Two is what comes after. When the silence is broken, the partners regain inner contact very quickly. They are at ease with each other and not at each other's throats. And even if the breeze grows to gale force, the partners sail bravely into the teeth of the wind because they have learned to sail together.

The first few times the doldrums hit are the most scary. After that, the partners begin to trade on their growing confidence that they do have a good thing going. They learn to go about their business without letting the depression grow desperate. They learn to respect each other's low times and allow each other breathing space. They learn to expect that the doldrums will hit periodically. Instead of anxious lulls, doldrums are okay-but-wish-they-were-over phases in the mutuality of Stage Four in the marriage journey.

One more feature of Stage Four requires attention: squalls. Yes, even in Stage Four there can be sudden, fierce squalls that unsettle and toss us about. Anger flares; words parry and thrust. But again there are major differences between a Stage Four squall and the tempests of previous stages. The squall is sudden and unexpected; most storms are predictable (even if we sometimes are blind to the signs). Most importantly, squalls are brief interludes and when a squall is over, it is over. Storms can hang around for a long time, circle back, and hit us again.

Partners in Stage Four learn to cope with conflict in less stormy ways than is typically the case in earlier stages. They do not allow disagreements to color the entire relationship for days. They no longer nurse real or imagined hurts into smouldering resentments. They let go of grudges, forgive, forget, and go on. When the dispute is over, like a squall, it is over.

In Stage Four, we no longer take conflicts as personal attacks that pervade the relationship for weeks. In fact, once we begin to experience that squalls interrupt but do not destroy our intimacy, we are able to face them head on without evasion or deceit. Even when we capsize, we no longer panic, for we know how to right the marriage craft.

7. Stage Five: Co-Creativity

> We can now recognize that the fate of the soul is the fate of the social order; that if the spirit within us withers, so too will all the world we build about us.
>
> — THEODORE ROSZAK

Mutuality is the tone and color of Stage Four. The intimacy each couple yearns for and struggles to achieve is an experienced reality. We have been able to receive, cherish, and nourish God's gift of intimacy in marriage. And the passing years give promise of an ongoing process of deepening intimacy as the partners become older, retire, and face the end of life together. Is there any need to talk of another major stage? Why not simply see the continuing growth and development as phases of Mutuality?

Maybe that is the way we should look at it. It certainly is true that an ongoing intimate marriage will continue to be marked by mutuality. Moreover, as suggested by our sequential model in which earlier stages point to later stages and later build on to earlier, creativity will be a feature of the earlier stages. Perhaps what I see as the co-creative stage overlaps for many couples with Stages Two through Four. Nevertheless, I want to suggest that it is helpful to speak of a fifth stage in marriage, the stage of the more pronounced energy of co-creativity.

FREE TO BE CLOSE AND APART

In Stage Three partners come to realize and to own what each is contributing to the sabotage of intimacy. In the mutuality of Stage Four partners begin to discover new ways to be together and begin to experience genuine intimacy. We are free to be near and free to be far. No longer smothered by closeness, we are able to breathe and love together. Two persons, we are at ease in being one. In giving myself, I receive myself back enlarged. Filled with a sense of well-being, enjoying being-with another, I experience a surge of power in knowing that I make a difference. And I go my way rejoicing. No longer devastated by separation, I am free to be far. Connected with self, interconnected with another self, we are empowered to fulfill our calling to love God and neighbor. The joy of mutuality flows over into caring for and sharing with all of God's creatures. The partners become "co-creators of newness—in themselves, their children, and in broader areas and relationships."[1]

THE CREATIVE RELEASE

It is this surge of co-creativity that marks the fifth stage of marriage. Our life rhythm of intimacy and identity comes to a new and final flourish. Nourished in intimacy, our love overflows. Secure in ourselves and in our intimate relationship, we have an abundant flow of energy for action in the world at large.

Mutuality releases power for creativity. When we no longer need to spend energy in keeping our illusions alive, when we no longer have to expend ourselves in trying to keep ourselves together, we surge with new energy. Most of us simply do not realize the incredible amount of energy we spend in keeping our masks on, playing our games, denying and projecting. When we learn to give up these illusions of control and own our negativity, the energy released for creative surges is surprising, almost unbelievable.

When in mutuality we learn to be at ease in each other's presence, our energy is replenished rather than diminished. Letting go of our masks and defenses, we are released to letting be. Letting be together is the healing communion of love that releases us to be present to ourselves and to our partner. And we are also released to be present in deepened ways to the rest of society and to the universe at large. It is this outreach of intimacy into the world that marks what I call the stage Co-Creativity.

CHARLENE AND VINCENT

Charlene and Vincent are a couple in their early fifties. They were married in the late fifties just before the women's liberation movement began to emerge. Charlene, who had adopted her father's model of assertiveness, independence, and creativity, could not tolerate playing the submissive, dependent role expected of women in the small town where she grew up. So Charlene married Vincent to escape. However, she didn't realize how deeply the traditional submissive, dependent feelings were embedded in her psyche. She vacillated between feeling dependent and independent. When she felt dependent, she wanted Vincent to be a caring parent. When she felt independent, every supportive move Vincent made to be intimate felt like invasion. Vincent became thoroughly confused. Being a pleaser, he tried to be as close or as distant as the situation demanded, but he never seemed to gauge the situation just right. Life became an endless power struggle in which Vincent felt rejected and Charlene felt isolated and abandoned. For the first fifteen years both Charlene and Vincent turned to career interests to find fulfillment. However, Charlene felt increasingly abandoned and alone. She longed for inner connection and intimacy with Vincent, but she lacked the self-awareness to be able to articulate these needs directly. She thought she wanted out. For his part, Vincent was more and more feeling like an intimacy-failure whose life was sinking into the gray mists of depression.

Fortunately, Charlene and Vincent sought help before ending their relationship. Charlene was challenged to know herself before taking any drastic action. Vincent was urged to confront his own "pleasing" and to be in touch with his own needs and wishes. Both entered upon painful but exhilarating journeys to self-awareness and identity. Charlene learned to accept both her dependent and independent sides. Rather than hoping Vincent will intuit her needs, she is learning to own them and make them known. Rather than needing to always intuit Charlene's needs, Vincent is learning to let his true rather than his pleasing self show.

Charlene and Vincent are now quite different from the people they were when they married over twenty years ago. They have learned to accept and value their own and each other's strengths and weaknesses. Sharing a common vision, they have separate careers that demand a great deal of energy, time, and creativity. Listening, encouraging, and supporting each other, they share the challenges of their work and relationships. At the same time, they both feel free to pursue their own interests and relationships in their own way. Having given up the illusion that marriage can fulfill all their needs, they have mutual and separate friends who enrich them individually and as a couple. They set aside regular times to get away and focus on their intimacy needs as a couple. Each feels grounded in being alone and in their mutuality together. Joyfully and creatively they seek to affirm and enrich their own lives and the lives of others.

PROCREATORS

An early sign of creativity in many marriages is the creation of a family. Children are a natural overflow of the mutuality of love. Often children are born in Stage Two and inadvertently get involved in the power struggle between parents. Our society even encourages young couples to have children in the hope of stabilizing their relationship. Too often the busyness of nurturing children puts the underlying dynamics of the marriage on hold for years. Intimacy needs that should be met by the partner are diverted to the children for fulfillment. Mommy has her "little man." Daddy adores his "little princess." In the process the children are the victims.

In all kinds of subtle and not so subtle ways the children may become the battleground for the parents' unresolved issues. Soon, however, they catch on and themselves become able protagonists in the fray. They sense what each of the parents wants to hear and doesn't want to hear. They learn how to play one parent off the other. The parents pass on to their children, to the third and fourth generation, their masks and defenses, their games and projections. We were not only shaped and formed in our mother's womb; the structure of our personality was formed and shaped in the crucible of the family. All of the defenses we struggle so valiantly to unlearn in later life we came by honestly in our earliest years.

The "empty nest" syndrome that afflicts many couples emphasizes the way family concerns may be used to avoid resolving the relationship issues typical of Stages Two and Three. The "empty nest" crisis produces clinging, emptiness, and depression; it especially strikes mothers who have overinvested in their families and it is a time when father and mother need to face each other squarely as husband and wife. Some parents try to hang on to the kids to put off the inevitable a while longer. Others throw themselves into their hobbies or causes to circumvent the showdown. Many fall into an affair rather than face themselves. Some simply pack up and leave without a word.

This is not meant to be discouraging, but it does happen. A family can be more of a place of rest and unconditional love—the birthright of every child—the more the marriage is a place of rest and unconditional love. When marriage is a life sentence, it stands to reason that the family will be too; it will rob rather than foster individuality.

What stands out clearly is that those of us who have children in Stage Two—most of us, perhaps—must not avoid working on our own relationship. Marriage and family are two interrelated but separate institutions. Each father and mother deserve to take a break together as husband and wife without the children. Moreover, it becomes clear that all of us, individually and as a society, need to do much more to help young couples arrive at the stage of Mutuality much earlier in the course of their marriages. Therein lies the greatest promise for loving and caring families unencumbered with all the family-of-origin baggage. In my view we could go a long way to improving the situation by setting up special support programs for couples who are just entering the power struggle stage.

During the intoxication of courtship and romance, couples are not so ready to hear about differences, masks, and unresolved issues from childhood. The situation changes dramatically as couples run into their differences and get locked into a power struggle. This would seem to be the optimum time for special seminars and support and therapy groups. With skilled and supportive assistance much of the hurt and pain members of the couple inflict on each other and their children (the memories of which later become such an obstacle to healing) could be avoided. In this way perhaps passage through the bogs and sandbars of Power Struggle on to the clearer waters of Mutuality and Co-Creativity could be more rapid. I suspect that many if not most young couples would welcome such support. At present there are not only many couples who hesitate to get married because they feel ill-prepared, there are also many who choose not to be parents because they don't want to inflict their hang-ups on their children.

There are, of course, a number of excellent marriage enrichment courses presently available. The Catholic church has pioneered in this area with Marriage Encounter. And more and more Protestant churches have developed programs. Such seminars reach thousands of couples, but, as we all know, the need is much greater. What I would like to see is as many counseling centers as gas stations—visible symbols that we care for people as much as we care for our cars. The allocation of resources for such enlarged marriage enrichment programs is, in my view, a number-one priority. We can afford nothing less. Only when we as co-creators in the family of God create families of intimates rather than collusions of strangers is the cause of justice and peace able to take root and flourish in our global family, for it is in the family that we bodily learn (or do not learn) our first and most deeply ingrained lessons about love and care, sacrifice and promise, wonder and adventure. It is the family that gives us our first name and first place.

THE OUTREACH OF INTIMACY

The gift of intimacy in marriage is for the mutual enjoyment of the partners, but it is not given only for the benefit of the couple, or even for the family. Love cannot be dammed up or boxed in. In fact, when couples turn in on themselves, it is a sign less of the flowering of their love than of its insecurity. Love, wherever it is found, seeks to flow outward in streams of healing.

Of course, as we have seen, it will be necessary at certain stages for couples to concentrate much of their energies on their relationship. Especially in Stage Two, throwing most of our energies in other projects can be an evasive, compulsive maneuver designed to hide our lack of intimacy. Nevertheless, when a marriage in Stage Four does not move beyond mutuality into co-creativity, it is an indication that some important issues remain unresolved.

Love, once experienced in its depth and troth, frees us to other acts of love and justice. To try to keep love just for us—the world be damned—is to kill it slowly. Trying to dam the outward flow of love disrupts its rhythm, whether in the freeze of boredom or the drowning of claustrophobia. We are not made just for each other; we are called to a ministry of love to everyone we meet and in all we do. In marriage too, Jesus' words hold true: in saving our lives we lose them, and in losing our lives in love to others, we drink of life more deeply.

A mark of mutuality is relinquishing our need to overinvest (or underinvest) in our marriage. Overinvestment traps the partners and smothers spontaneity and creativity. A co-creative relationship, of course, requires investment in the marriage (and in the family). But to retain its vitality and zest, it also requires investment in persons and projects outside of itself. The co-creative couple develops a web of meaningful interrelationships— work, church, recreation, friendships, citizen groups, art groups, and so on—that support the marriage and deepen its joys.

FRIENDSHIP

Loving is not restricted to marriage and family. Thank God. We all need acquaintances, comrades-in-arms, partners in business and leisure, companions for support and sharing. Cordial, supportive, and pleasant people make all the difference in the daily push and pull of life. Kind words and caring smiles lift our sad faces and lighten our heavy hearts. And then there are friends, those tried and true companions who are special beyond words.

In the mutuality and equality that mark Stage Four marriages, both partners have stopped projecting all their needs on each other. They no longer put all their eggs in the marital basket. Relieving marriage of the impossible burden of fulfilling all our needs and desires, we are freed to give and receive in other kinds of relationships. We can give time and energy to the cultivation of friendships, not as competitors to our marriage, but as healthy complements.

Again the matter of timing is important. Friendship has bad press and is rarely celebrated, because often in our experience it becomes a cover for a sexual affair. That can easily happen, especially when a marriage is stuck in Stage Two. Rather than facing ourselves, we are tempted to lose ourselves in sexual passion with a new person. That is not to suggest that true friends never develop a strong sexual attraction for each other; they often do. But then they need to work hard to keep their marriage and friendship separate for, as the experience of many bears witness, we ask for trouble when we confuse them. We also need to understand that a momentary lapse, if checked, is— though sad—not the end of the world or of the marriage. Such a crisis is an invitation for both of us to look beyond blaming— to soul searching, forgiving, and deeper intimacy. What is missing in our relationship that leads me to wander? What need is not being sufficiently met? What have I contributed to the problem? Emotional clearance can lead to new understandings and a renewed connection.

Friendship, it is true, is not without real dangers, but the alternative is worse: the prison of loneliness. This is especially true for the myriads of singles, but it is also true for the many marrieds who are trying to hold on to their marriages even though they are often bleak and lonely. Without friends, we can be so lonely that our need for contact propels us, almost unknowingly, into affairs. I remember the aching pain of a single woman who cried that she had not felt the touch of a human hand for over a month. Friendship is one of God's special antidotes to loneliness, a very special way to fill the human need for closeness, touch, and troth.

When two people know how to be full partners in marriage, they also know how to give and receive of themselves in the joys of friendship. Enlarged by my soul friends, I grow in my marriage. Nourished in my marriage, I am able to reach out to friends. Friendship and marriage work together.

DOING JUSTICE

Committed intimacy creates, nourishes, and flows out not only into the private arenas of family and friendships, but into the spheres of public commitment. The power of love needs to be directed to the care of the world and its creatures. "Justice," as one poster exclaimed, "not just us!" To love is to be a healer. To be one in our commitment to love and justice strengthens rather than weakens our bond of troth. Public involvements will be born not out of the frantic need to escape each other, but out of the gladness of full-hearted people who lift their eyes and behold the needs of the world.

The potential for healing is unquestionable. No longer needing to get into issues to inflate our egos or to project our hurts on society, our involvements can be nonmanipulative and healing. We will be able to caretake the world, working for a more just, more loving, people-first society. Freed in troth to reach out and develop other contacts and new talents, the partners return to their intimacy with new experiences to share and new opportunities for growth. The intimacy deepens, and the couple is empowered to reach out in new circles of caring. The couple develops an inward and outward rhythm, personal intimacy and societal renewal linked together in the reciprocity of compassion, which our broken world so badly needs.

Our world labors under the specter of nuclear war. It is burdened by the terrible weight of human suffering, racial discrimination, and economic exploitation. The earth and its inhabitants groan for deliverance, awaiting, as Paul exclaims in Romans 8:19, with eager expectation the revelation of the sons and daughters of God. It is especially those of us who have our souls and bodies nourished in the intimacy of marriage who need to look beyond the face of our beloved and see the flawed face of the world. With new zeal and energy we need to act as copartners with God in the ministry of healing, for it is to that mission that we were created and recreated in Jesus Christ.

The need of course is immense—so gigantic, so huge, that we can easily be overwhelmed and lose heart. Immobilized into passivity, we can easily become cynics, opportunists, profligates, or recluses. But God calls us only to do what our two hands find to do in our own backyard. We need not take on the whole world; that is God's terrain. However, as members of God's body we do each have our own limited, but unique, role to play in God's ministry of global reconciliation. We are called to co-creativity—as scientists, politicians, artists, teachers, plumbers, bakers, peacemakers, farmers, and so on. To hold at bay our own inclinations to depression and fatalism, each of us would do well to join in a project in which we could experience in bodily and tangible ways our power for healing.

Not only is it our global calling to be agents of change, re-forming structures of injustice and opposing all forms of violence, but such work is necessary for the continued existence of intimacy itself. The growth of troth takes awareness, ease, and time. However, faced with the mammoth problems of war, poverty, and ecology, millions of people can devote little if any time to the quality of their intimate relationships. Survival is the bottom line.

Nor may we forget that even in our countries and cities the ideologies of consumption and control in which people are second and things first have invaded and eroded the fabric of marriage and family. Machines are re-creating us in their image. The very institutions in which we live and grow are often themselves part of the problem. Instead of communions of love and healing, families and marriages turn into armed camps, microcosms of the world at large. Compassion has gone into exile. And so the problem comes home to each of us, for our personalities are formed in these institutions and through them the enemy takes root in our own souls.

CREATIVE INTIMACY WITH GOD

As the bond of intimacy in marriage matures and deepens, it stretches out beyond marriage. Marital intimacy opens us to a fuller sense of intimacy with all of the universe and with God as The Intimate, and a revitalized intimacy with God in turn strengthens our marriage. My life with my partner becomes an experience of the love of God; my life with God comes alive in my marriage. Communion with God and the faithful exercise of such communion is an important aspect of marriage in all its stages. At the same time, such unity with God, nature, and life can reach a new experiential level of harmony and fulfillment in the fifth stage of marriage.

Although always an important dimension of marriage, a deeper sense of the meaning and reality of faith emerges in the co-creative stage. It is especially then that a couple looks for ways to experience the belonging they have together in increasingly wider circles. Individually and as a couple they yearn for that belonging on a universe-wide scale: how can we be at home and belong in this big world? Ultimately, we need to ground our intimacy in the creative and re-creative intimacy of the Creator God. We all belong together in sacred covenant, humans, animals, trees, rocks, planets—all the family of creatures—and God.

In fact, as we have had opportunity to notice, it is our failure, in the first months of life, to develop this "basic trust" (Erikson) that makes it so difficult for us to be intimate with each other as adults. It is this same lack that twists our urge to share into the compulsion to master. It undermines for many of us a full experience of God's love. Conversely, when we do achieve intimacy with another person, our sense of connection with other people, with nature, and with God is renewed and transformed. A couple's intimacy is not complete until it is rooted in a greater and deeper cohabitation with all of creation and the God of creation.

Connection with self (identity), connection with others (intimacy), connection with all of God's creatures (solidarity), connection with God (faith) together make up the spirituality of life. To experience such interconnections in the midst of the brokenness is to participate in the birth of a new world in which peace and justice shall dwell. We can but tremble at the awesome responsibility of being co-creators with God, "wounded healers."

COMPETING VISIONS

The outreach of intimacy beyond marriage is often as good for the marriage as it is for the larger world, but, regrettably, this is not always the case. If a couple reaching out does not share ultimate values, their relationship itself will become strained and tense. Coping with competing visions of life is difficult in any community; it is doubly so in marriage. The problem escalates when the couple does not share the same faith. Shared celebration of life in a communion of faith is a most important ingredient in the deepening of marital intimacy.

The problem is not individual differences or divergent interests. Although these often are a focus of conflict particularly in Stage Two, troth thrives on the unique identities of the partners. This becomes especially apparent as the couple journeys into the mutuality of Stages Four and Five. In the mutuality of a common commitment, individual differences give spark and shine to a relationship. On the other hand, if we have exactly the same likes and dislikes, the same thoughts and feelings, if we disagree about nothing, the relationship will be pedestrian and boring.

The problem emerges when there is disagreement about the overall perspective and ultimate meanings in terms of which we develop our special gifts. If partners in troth are at odds about the fundamental meaning of life, it demands an unusual degree of maturity as well as a high degree of commitment to achieve creative closeness. Some couples try to avoid facing this basic disagreement.

A much better approach is to build on the mutual respect that is ours and to learn to communicate about the basic disagreements. If partners can avoid pressuring each other to change and convert, a way of relating can develop that need not jeopardize intimacy. It is not problems in themselves that are devastating to a relationship; it is the distance they create between the partners. Ongoing communication keeps up the indispensable contact and keeps open the search for a common spiritual ground. It is when we feel fully and unconditionally accepted as the person we are that we are most open to change. It is when we experience that the other person is behind us, no questions asked, that we take most seriously what he or she believes. And if, moreover, we are deeply committed to living with our partner, an impetus develops that induces us to arrive at a common understanding of life that transcends certain basic differences.

Understanding, acceptance, and willingness to learn are not the only gifts we owe each other, but they are at the same time the best channels for resolving basic worldview differences. As a couple journeys together they will usually find the need to revise their understanding of the faith by which they live. As their relationship grows in freedom and intimacy, so will grow their need for a worldview that supports this journey. This interactional dynamic offers the best hope that a couple who continues to struggle together will be able to find themselves in a common vision.

INTIMACY, NOT ALIENATION

Marriage, I am saying, is not all of life, nor dare we make it into all, for then it becomes an idol that is sure to devour us. Accepting the gift of what we have together, we are called as individuals and as a partnership to foster our gifts in the societal pursuit of justice and mercy for all. Our com-passion is to flow into compassion and healing everywhere. The challenge is mind-boggling. But living out of the Promises of God, our co-promising is a promise of healing for the world. Nourished and refreshed in our intimacy, we gain resources to spend on behalf of the world and its needs. The peace and hope born in our intimacy translates into power to become agents of healing in our society. Co-creative, we are empowered to be full partners in the Healing Mission of the Creator. Intimacy flows outward into works of justice and mercy. And it is only as we experience acceptance, forgiveness, kindness, and healing in our intimacies of marriage, family, and friendship, that mercy and peace have a realistic chance of extending into the global community at large.

Intimacy, not alienation, is the fundamental fact of life. That is the good news of reconciliation. In the Spirit of Christ we may rise above the domination/submission/alienation syndrome that has invaded the creation and taken us hostage even in our own families and marriages. Establishing global peace and harmony in the name of Immanuel, God-with-Us, begins with a renewed commitment to a people-first, things-second ethos of love. An ethic of love can halt the dismantling of our families, marriages, and friendships inspired by the dominant cultural myths of one-upmanship, mastery, and competition. When intimacy is rekindled in the hearth of marriage, when the family is a school for compassion, when the tender plant of friendship is nourished, we will have the heart to care and the faith to persevere in our mission of hope and healing for the world.

8. The Ongoing Journey

We are speaking of love. A leaf, a handful of seed—
    begin with these, learn a little what it is to love.
First, a leaf, a fall of rain, then someone to receive
    what a leaf has taught you, what a fall of
    rain has ripened.
No easy process, understand; it could take a
    lifetime, it has mine, and still I've never mastered it—

                                                —TRUMAN CAPOTE

Intimacy is an ongoing journey. As long as there is life, there will be growth and change. I have described the journey in five successive stages, each with its own unique opportunities and challenges. To understand these stages is to be prepared for them. New understandings make possible new ways of being together.

It is hoped that studying the rough maps and charts laid out in this book has given us a better sense of where we are and where we need to go. We have identified where we struggle and where we are stuck and have even felt a sense of relief that we are not alone. We have sensed anew that we do want to change; we long for healing. We may have been able to resolve old hurts, sense new possibilities, and develop our sense of identity and intimacy. But we may also feel discouraged. We have tried to change before, but it hasn't worked. We wish to change and learn new ways of navigating, but bad habits are difficult to break. Especially when the going gets rough and the breakers roar, we tend to slip back into old patterns and repeat the old mistakes. Dare we hope that things can really be different?

In this last chapter I want to encourage us to continue to seek and find help. It contains no recipe for success, no guarantees—there are no such things. Each couple must sail on their own, finding their own way. But it helps to have a map, and it helps even more to sense the support of other couples making the same journey. And it can be especially helpful when we have the assistance of pilots who have sailed these waters before. Some things can be done to dispel the mist. There are ways to enhance intimacy and nourish love. And once we experience the warmth of healing, something in us expands and we are never the same again.

THE WILL TO CHANGE

First and foremost, the will to change must be present and active. And that is not as simple or as obvious as it sounds. Often we pay lip service to our desire to change. "Of course, I want to change. Who do you think I am?" What we mean is that we are all for change on our terms, when it is convenient, and when the results are guaranteed. But if it means changing ourselves, owning our inadequacies, exposing our vulnerable flanks, we are no longer interested, thank you. Or we begin the process and run into our recalcitrant natures. "I tried, but it didn't work. I can't change." Fear grips our soul and we retrench. We see no other way out. Or perhaps we have made some progress and then suffer a relapse (as most often happens). "It won't work, anyway." We panic. Or we refuse to really give ourselves to the process because of our fear of the unknown, a terror we all know too well. Some of us struggle with inertia. We are burned out and simply have no energy.

Change and growth is risky. It always brings turmoil with it. It often seems easier to stay where we are than to risk movement. The risk of intimacy is especially unsettling because it involves exposing the inner recesses of our soul. Most of us prefer the predictable routes and routines instead of the insecurity of uncharted waters. What we often don't realize is that to settle for safety in a world where change is natural is to risk depression and boredom!

Even when the will to change is present and accounted for, it is often squelched by our defensive routines and the illusory masks. But if we can find ways to go beneath our masks and face our self, we can trust that change will really come. Then we become enablers, agents of change who can actively choose our own future and reach out to others, rather than continue to exist as victims of our past, in retreat from the future.

TRIGGER EVENTS

We all frequently experience trigger events, events that unsettle us because they penetrate beneath our masks and remind us of unresolved issues from the past. It may be the loss of a job, sickness in the family, or an argument with a friend that sends us reeling. Trigger events may be very little things. Maybe we find ourselves flying into a rage for no apparent reason. Maybe we look in the mirror and realize that we look like a little boy abandoned by Mother. Someone smiles at us and we are sure that we are being laughed at. We lose our way in a crowd or forget where we parked our car and suddenly our stomach knots in panic. We all have such tender places and trigger events remind us of their presence.

Trigger events can also remind us of unrealized potentials or unknown gifts. We hear from a friend how much our caring was appreciated. We suddenly have to chair a meeting and discover that we have a knack for it. We are "forced" to find our own way and discover an ability to make it on our own. We are invited to try our hand at painting and are surprised by the results. One with our spouse in our concern for our sick child, we experience a precious moment of meeting in the middle.

All of us have such tender places of unresolved hurts or unrealized gifts. They need care, and somewhere deep down we want to care for them. But it's far from easy. Most often we avoid looking. And even when an experience triggers our awareness, too often we quickly move to obliterate the awareness. We put our masks back in place. It's like carefully bandaging an infection, which never really gets much better from year to year. Afraid to discover what the trigger event is telling us, we prefer the pretense of covering over. After all, our masks have allowed us to survive rather comfortably for a long while.

Since the masks have become second nature to us, we hardly realize that, although they may defend us against hurt, they also prevent genuine healing and mutual vulnerability. We don't want to hear that our defensive masks are illusions, addictions upon which we depend, without which we feel undone and unable to continue. Locked into our illusions, we are not free to follow through on any will to change.

BREAKTHROUGHS

Illusions, like addictions, are difficult to break, but they can be broken. The reality of trigger events is clear evidence that our deepest needs and desires continue to reveal themselves in our daily lives. What we require is help and support so that we can allow the trigger events to give birth to breakthrough experiences.

In the first place, new understandings that life *can* be different are a tremendous impetus for change. People often lack the nerve to change because they don't know what it means. Why get excited about something that can't happen anyway? But when we know that things don't have to be the way they are, hope for change can take root in our hearts. Knowing that the conflicts of Stage Two are a necessary passage to the intimacy of later stages helps us to stay with the process instead of seeking to mask the reality that our relationship is very troubled. Knowing that angers and fears, when owned, paradoxically give way to hope and healing encourages us to face the despair and pain. Knowing that the panic of being without defenses, naked and helpless, is a stage in the rebirth of the self assures us that there is life after death. Guided by the rough and ready map of marriage offered in these pages, we can have a sense of where we are and some sense of where we need to go. Now, perhaps we can afford to admit that we are stuck at a certain place. And owning our stuck position is the necessary beginning of getting unstuck.

Knowledge encourages us to take advantage of the trigger events we experience. Maybe we are stunned by the sudden rage that seethes within. Perhaps we are caught in a breach of trust, or we are faced with the loss of a spouse. After the initial impact, which may last from a moment to a few days or even weeks, we act in typical ways to deny the emerging reality: "I don't want to talk about it"; "I'm sorry, that's just the way I am"; "I'm okay.

I can handle it"; "There must be a mistake; it can't be true"; and on and on.

Denial is a predictable and normal first response, but often we persist in our denial, calling on all the resources of our defenses to wipe the experience from our memory. We deny our feelings, throw ourselves into our routines and go on as usual. In so doing we squander the opportunity for growth and healing. Of course, it is more difficult to persist in denial when, as in a loss through death or divorce, the empty chair is a stark reminder of the reality. But even then we may numb our feelings, fall into depression, act the passive martyr, and try to escape internalizing the loss. After a while, we go on with our lives. But we succeed in covering over rather than deeply accepting and resolving the loss. The unresolved anger, guilt, and despair have not gone away and will no doubt erupt spontaneously under some later stress.

Instead of lingering in denial, we need to be encouraged—and we need to encourage others—to let go of our defensive armoring and let ourselves down into the anger, guilt, fear, or sadness. That is the route to healing. The anger is there, the fear is real, the sadness is palpable, whether we like it or not. Until we own our anger, it owns us. Until we acknowledge our fear, it keeps us in bondage. Until we touch our sadness, it keeps us in its iron grip. Not owning our feelings is to be victimized by them. But owning our negative feelings and emotions is the way we can release ourselves from their power. This is one of the truly liberating paradoxes of life.

To deny our emotions or to repress them is to remain in their power. Emotions refuse to be silenced. If we fail to deal with them, instead of going away they arrest us, closing down the whole process of human growth. When we refuse to listen to our feelings, we lose contact with ourselves and with reality. We begin to operate as-if, defensively, and our perceptions become distorted. Very often we blame, project, and rationalize. Out of contact with our inner self, we are limited in the intimacy we can experience with another person. If we repress our feelings of guilt, we will never really be able to enjoy ourselves without reservation, for we will keep our subconscious need to punish ourselves. Emotional withholding or repressing takes its toll as we hunch our shoulders, knot our stomachs, or tighten our jaws. Our eyes may burn without physical cause or our heads may ache with internal tension. On the other hand, when we own our moods and feelings, they begin to lose their power. We are no longer so afraid of feelings that we have to deny them. We are able to take responsibility for them and for ourselves. In allowing ourselves to feel what we feel, we begin the process of integrating our feelings in our lives. And letting go and allowing ourselves to be, we are surprised at the flow of energy. We feel alive, even if sometimes in extreme pain. The enormous energy formerly invested in maintaining our defenses is suddenly available for more constructive purposes.

The process of turning disturbing trigger events into healing breakthroughs seems to follow much the same developmental sequence that Elizabeth Kübler-Ross describes in her stages of coming to an acceptance of death. After the *denial*, there is the *anger* of "Why me?" The anger passes into *bargaining*: "Okay, but . . ." Then there is a *resignation* leading finally to *acceptance*. Letting ourselves down into our feelings and facing our deep hurts is to set aside our doing and accept our being. But it is just our deeply felt dis-ease in our being that led us and leads us to find ourselves in our doing. So we go through a period of denial rather than face the deepest fears unprotected, completely exposed. We resist the only way we know, the ways we learned when we were infants.

If we are able to stay in touch and trust the process, we admit our anger and fear, but we tend to place the onus outside of ourselves: "If only you weren't . . ." Then we get in touch with the deep despair that we will never be accepted and loved for ourselves. Finally, we give up trying to hold off the despair and we descend into pain and fear. We own our terror, our fear, our hurt, our rage, our humiliation, our helplessness, our frustration. We let go and let be what will be. In the experience of acceptance, release occurs—sometimes suddenly, sometimes slowly, sometimes almost unawares. It is in such transforming experiences, the culmination of a process, that we break through to another level of existence. Fearing the end, we experience a new beginning. Letting go of our defenses (which we are confident hold our lives together) becomes the passage to finding and accepting ourselves. We see ourselves as we really are, with our limitations and our gifts. Seeing ourself as the person we are, we are able to see other persons for who they are. The courage to be gives us the power to become. The pain of self-discovery gives way to the joy of new wholeness.

True personal identity emerges through a series of such break-throughs integrating all the different aspects of a person's life. Often it is only in retrospect that we can describe what happened in the process; certainly only over time do we experience the full significance of the experiences. In the process we face our need to repent of our attempts at self-security and we are invited to accept our ground in the Source of all that is. For it is, ultimately, the Love of God that "lets us be." Dwelling in that letting-be, we are empowered to "let be," face, accept, and change ourselves. Easter follows Good Friday. Dawn is born in the darkness. The faces of the void, says Kierkegaard, become the faces of God.

DIS-IDENTIFICATION AND REINTEGRATION

Breakthrough experiences can be as many and as varied as there are persons to have them. Any experience can trigger the process leading to breakthrough. It may be a moment of quiet in the woods in which our perception of the self and world changes. It may happen in the ecstasy of creating a poem, a sculpture, or a painting. It may be the moment in which we feel the presence of another. What such experiences do seem to have in common is a new sense of connection within ourselves in spite of the brokenness. It is the taste of the real.

As we increasingly accept rather than reject the be-ing we truly are, we see ourselves more clearly. We are able to take distance and dis-identify with some of our roles and defensive postures that have cut us off from intimacy with self and others. We are able to nurture parts of our self that we have left buried and unattended. We are able to go back and care for the tender and hurt places. When we no longer find security in our doing; the drive to take refuge in "pleasing," "defying," or "avoiding" becomes less attractive. We realize that the old ways only covered over our chronic dissatisfaction with the way things were. Becoming more and more disillusioned with the illusions by which we have lived, we find that they lose their hold on our lives. We experience new freedom to choose and an amazing power to begin to forge new ways.

Breakthroughs turn things around. They mark the owning of the old, which opens the way to reconciliation and newness. Instead of running from myself, I face myself. Facing myself, repenting, experiencing forgiveness and acceptance in the Spirit of God, I am able to move out in forgiveness to others. Compassion becomes my way of being in the world. And intimacy becomes possible.

The change from the old ways of alienation to the new ways of compassion is slow and turbulent. The old cultural ideals and the old ways of behaving die slowly. Nevertheless change can and does come. And the possibility for change is greatly enhanced when we become aware of a vision offering a different kind of reality. Until that point we don't dare know what we know. And even when we know another way, the road to intimacy and wholeness is strewn with obstacles within and without. Nevertheless, the special moments in which we know things are different grab hold of us and do not let go. A felt-body experience of new growth and life makes us less tolerant of the old, and it creates a hunger for more. Big things begin small: a man lets down and is vulnerable; a woman takes in that she is being treated as an equal. Moments of meeting in the middle give us glimpses of being new creatures in Jesus Christ. Intimacy with self and others is a beckoning hope and a growing reality because intimacy, not alienation, is the fundamental truth of the universe.

SEEKING AND FINDING HELP

Changing means taking advantage of the trigger events in our lives, listening more carefully to our internal sounds. We need to guard against the calluses that grow so easily over the sore points in our close relationships. Gently we need to probe our attitudes. Difficult as it is, it is the only way to keep our relations from growing stale, dull, and defensive.

But what if we are bogged down in such a stale, dull, and defensive relationship? What about those of us in pain, despite our brave facades? What about those of us who feel a growing desperation or those of us who are going through the motions, afraid that we have no feelings? What can we do?

We can begin by admitting what we really feel to ourselves—without blaming ourselves or our partner—and committing ourselves to take action. Even this little first step is important. The fear of acknowledging the truth is itself debilitating. A promise to act brings its own relief. At least something is bound to happen.

In the second place, we can share our feelings with our partner, again without blame or rancor. This too is a bold step. Sometimes a partner has too much invested to admit the truth and denies that anything is wrong. Or he or she may dump on us or wallow in guilt. But at least we have been honest and reached out. Often a partner experiences in and through his or her own sadness a deep surge of relief. What he or she had felt but had not been able to share we have finally expressed. In fact, what happens then is the first intimation of intimacy. We are honoring each other with the truth as we experience it.

The longer a couple puts off acknowledging their situation the more difficult the situation becomes. And the more difficult it becomes to recognize the situation for what it is. For that reason every couple from the beginning of their relationship needs to take great pains to make sure that every week they have a time of intimate sharing, checking each other's perceptions, expectations, and experiences. Five to ten minutes of sitting knee to knee, eye to eye, open heart to open heart, sharing where they are together, works wonders. Truly, an ounce of preventive intimacy is worth a pound of marital therapy.

Finally, we can resolve to seek help in rebuilding our relationship. It is important that the partners are of one mind in seeking help. If one partner drags his or her heels, therapy is made doubly difficult. It is well to note that asking for such help is more a sign of strength than an admission of failure. It takes genuine courage to admit a problem and reach out for help.

This help can take various forms. Each couple needs to find what is best for their needs. If they choose counseling, the counselor must be someone with whom they feel comfortable and can develop a relationship of trust. A first step could be enrolling in a marriage enrichment seminar or going to a short-term marriage counselor. We can ask friends for their recommendations or consult with our pastor. It will soon become apparent if longer-term therapy is indicated.

The importance of dealing with problems as they arise is so important that I believe every couple, in the early years, should be encouraged to "air out" their relationship with a trusted counselor at least once a year. At present couples often come for help when the train, so to speak, is already down the tracks. We take our cars in for one-thousand-, five-thousand-, and ten-thousand-mile checkups—why not our marriages?

For couples in serious distress longer-term therapy is likely indicated. Supporting each other rather than setting off each other's defenses will grow on us. Even if the partners are convinced the marriage is over, counseling is imperative—if for no other reason than gaining insight into what went wrong. And even if it becomes clear that divorce will be liberation from the prison of an embattled marriage, counseling is in order to help the couple disentangle and separate. For until such emotional separation takes place, any new relationship begins encumbered with the old. The old partners need time and help to free themselves from the old ties. Often, as we have noticed throughout this book, the relationship is in disrepair because as individuals we are out of touch with ourselves. In such cases individual therapy is also highly recommended. Psychotherapy has proved for many to be a good road to healing. There is an amazing array of psychotherapies from which to choose: talk therapies such as psychoanalysis, rational-emotive therapy, or Rogerian client-centered therapy; bodily expressive therapies such as bioenergetics, gestalt therapy, or primal therapy; behavioral therapy; existential therapy; and dream, art or music therapy.

SPIRITUAL PSYCHOTHERAPY

Why do I recommend psychotherapy? Not because it is a cure-all; it is not. The best psychotherapist cannot change anyone; we need to change ourselves. But changing ourselves requires focused concentration on ourselves uncluttered by the demands of our roles. We need to be able to stop dead in our tracks, take distance, and look and listen at our internal sights and sounds. We need to learn the art of introspection. In our busy society such times of silence and awakening are at a premium. In fact many of us are so programmed that we either run ourselves ragged or we vegetate. The ability to set aside our daily business and to meditate, penetrating to our deepest center, is for many impossible. But it is through meditation involving our whole persons that we descend into our depths, escape our overcrowded minds and discover the center of our personality and the Ground of our being. Then, in touch with the truth of who we are, we may be transformed.

In a culture where such attention to self is suspect and in a culture where the mediative art of being-with-self is largely lost, it is a matter of great urgency that we find ways to learn this lost art. Retreats as oases for the cultivation of the inner life are one excellent and fortunately growing possibility. But many of us are unable or too fearful to make the inward journey on our own. We need a guide, a mentor, a spiritual director, or a therapist to accompany us and support us in the inner journey.

Psychotherapy is one excellent way in which a person may be helped to probe the inner depths. A skilled psychotherapist can help us renurture ourselves; he or she can guide us and accompany us through the dark night of the soul. Since facing the radical questions about our inner being involves, at the same time, the question about the Source and Ground of our being, we are best helped by a psychotherapist who sees the deeply spiritual nature of the work. Or if we are working with a spiritual director, we will likely benefit the most by one who sees the deeply psychological nature of the work.

Since so much depends on the trust between therapist and client, it is also crucial that we find a person with whom we "click." We need to look for a psychotherapist who is profoundly spiritual and profoundly personal, a therapist who shares (or at least respects) our fundamental values and faith, and a therapist to whom we feel personally attracted. We are best served by "shopping around" for the right therapist with as much care as we normally employ in the purchase of a new house or car. In the right situation and with the proper commitment to the inner work, individual psychotherapy, which may last three or more years, is able to nurture the kind of breakthroughs that make a major difference in our personal lives and our relationships.

Such therapy demands a large investment of time and money. But if our hurts were inflicted in the first years of life, we have had years to perfect our defenses. No wonder it takes us, even with skilled help, a number of years to dismantle the defenses or at least to adjust them to serve our best interests. Personal experience needs to lead the way. If we sense change, even if it is slow and even if we relapse in periods of stress, we will begin to taste the rewards of increased intimacy with self, others, and God. That is my experience and the experience of many others.

Coming to a deepened sense of self spills over into our relations with others. Marital therapy can help us work out a new way of being with our partner. There are yet other ways to receive assistance. We can join support groups or therapy groups. We can nurture friendships with persons who have the same goals, desires, and passions. We can approach our church and let them know of our interest in being a member of a small sharing community. Perhaps we are called to be the mover in the establishment of such a group.

AN INVITATION

Intimacy is an open and inviting voyage. It is a gift from God that is an invitation to joy and gladness. This book provides a beginning map for our use on the Seas of Marriage. Along with other navigational aids and looking to troth as our North Star, we are invited to chart our own voyages of self-discovery into intimacy with self, others, the creation, and God. We begin where we are. Nothing more is asked but the willingness to prepare and venture out, ultimately; we have nothing to fear. For in the light of the Advent, life is an adventure to deepening intimacy and wholeness. If we need the help of guides and pilots (the seas are stormy), help is for the asking. For those just starting out, Bon Voyage! For those already in passage, Take Heart! For in the fear-and-trembling passage of intimacy, the God of Love is with us; we are not alone.

Notes

CHAPTER 1

1. Matthew Fox, *A Spirituality Named Compassion and the Healing of the Global Village, Humpty Dumpty and Us* (Minneapolis, MN: Winston Press, 1979), chap. 2.
2. See Luise Eichenbaum and Susie Orbach, *Understanding Women: A Feminist Psychoanalytic Approach* (New York: Basic Books, 1983), *What Do Women Want, Exploding the Myth of Dependency* (New York: Berkley Books, 1983), and Lillian Rubin, *Intimate Strangers: Men and Women Together* (New York: Harper & Row, 1983) for excellent discussions of the socialization process. See Carol Gilligan, *In a Different Voice* (Cambridge: Harvard University Press, 1982) for a discussion of the differences between male and female moral development.
3. Rubin, *Intimate Strangers*, 42–43.
4. See my essay, "Self or Society: Is There a Choice?" in Craig Ellison, ed., *Your Better Self: Christianity, Psychology and Self-Esteem* (San Francisco: Harper & Row, 1983) for a discussion of the interrelationship between personal growth and societal renewal.
5. See my earlier book, *I Pledge You My Troth* (San Francisco: Harper & Row, 1975) for a discussion of the nature of troth, particularly 20–22.
6. During the final stages of preparing this manuscript for publication, Susan M. Campbell's *The Couple's Journey: Intimacy as a Path to Wholeness* (San Luis Obispo, CA: Impact Publishers, 1980) came to my attention. Her book is a surprising complement to my own. She also identifies five stages and her stage names are remarkably similar to mine: Romance, Power Struggle, Stability, Commitment, Co-Creation. I take this amazing congruence as evidence that there must be something to our independent analyses!

CHAPTER 2

1. See Luise Eichenbaum and Susie Orbach, *What Do Women Want, Exploding the Myth of Dependency* (New York: Basic Books, 1983), chap. 2, "The Great Taboo: Men's Dependency."
2. For the correlation of grounding to the physical way our feet meet the

ground, see Alexander Lowen, *Depression and the Body: The Biological Basis of Faith and Reality* (Baltimore: Penguin, 1973), chap. 2, "Grounding in Reality."

3. Lillian Rubin, *Intimate Strangers: Men and Women Together* (New York: Harper & Row, 1983), 110.

4. Rubin, *Intimate Strangers*, 92.

5. See William Kilpatrick, *Identity and Intimacy* (New York: Dell, 1975) for an excellent discussion of the identity-intimacy relation.

6. M. Mahler, F. Pine, and A. Bergman, *The Psychological Birth of the Human Infant* (New York: Basic Books, 1975). For an engaging and more popular presentation, see Louise Kaplan, *Oneness and Separateness: From Infant to Individual* (New York: Simon & Schuster, 1978).

7. See Donald Evans, "Towards a Philosophy of Openness," in M. Faghfoury, *Analytical Philosophy of Religion in Canada* (Ottawa: University of Ottawa Press, 1982), 258–261 for a superb discussion of these dynamics.

8. See John J. Mitchell, *The Adolescent Predicament* (Toronto: Holt, Rinehart and Winston, 1975) for one readable account and Jay Haley, *Leaving Home: The Therapy of Disturbed Young People* (New York: McGraw-Hill, 1980) for an approach to adolescent therapy.

9. D. W. Winnicott, a British child psychiatrist, first introduced the concept of "the good-enough mother." See D. W. Winnicott, *The Family and Individual Development* (London: Tavistock, 1965), p. 17.

10. See Sam Keen, *The Passionate Life: Stages of Loving* (San Francisco: Harper & Row, 1983), chap. 5, "Rebellious Emotions and Twisted Adolescence." Keen's book is a fascinating and passionate analysis of the stages of human loving in interconnection with God and the whole cosmic web of life.

CHAPTER 4

1. Eric Berne, *Games People Play* (New York: Grove Press, 1964).

2. A number of books have taken up this theme. See, for example, James Rue and Louise Shanahan, *Daddy's Girl, Mama's Boy* (New York: Bobs-Merrill, 1978), Nancy Friday, *My Mother, My Self* (New York: Dell, 1977), Paul Olsen, *Sons and Mothers: Why Men Behave as They Do* (New York: M Evans, 1981), and Maggie Scarfe, *Unfinished Business* (Garden City, N.Y.: Doubleday, 1980).

CHAPTER 5

1. On letting pain be pain, see Matthew Fox, *Original Blessing* (Sante Fe, NM: Bear & Company, 1983), 140–148.

2. See James Loder, *The Transforming Moment* (New York: Harper & Row, 1981).

3. See Charlotte Clinebell, *Meet Me in the Middle: On Becoming Human Together* (New York: Harper & Row, 1973).

CHAPTER 6

1. See S. Miller, E. Nunnally, and D. Wachman, *Talking Together* (Minneapolis, MN: Interpersonal Communications Programs, 1979).

2. Miller, Nunnally, and Wachman, *Talking Together*, 52.

CHAPTER 7

1. Howard and Charlotte Clinebell, *The Intimate Marriage* (New York: Harper & Row, 1970), 197.

Selected Bibliography

Ables, Billie S. *Therapy for Couples*. San Francisco: Jossey-Bass, 1977.

Augsburger, David. *Caring Enough to Forgive*. Ventura, CA: Regal Books, 1981.

Bach, George, and Ronald Deutsch. *Pairing*. New York: Avon Books, 1970.

Bach, George, and Peter Wyden. *The Intimate Enemy*. New York: Avon Books, 1968.

Becker, Ernest. *The Denial of Death*. New York: The Free Press, 1973.

Berne, Eric. *Games People Play*. New York: Grove Press, 1964.

Bird, Joseph, and Lois Bird. *Marriage Is for Grownups*. Garden City, NY: Image Books, 1971.

Blanck, Rubin, and Gertrude Blanck. *Marriage and Personal Development*. New York: Columbia University Press, 1968.

Bockus, Frank. *Couple Therapy*. New York: Jason Aronson, 1980.

Buber, Martin. *I and Thou*. Translated by W. Kaufmann. New York: Scribner, 1970.

Campbell, Susan. *The Couple's Journey: Intimacy as a Path to Wholeness*. San Luis Obispo, CA: Impact Publishers, 1980.

Carter, Elizabeth A., and Monica McGoldrick, eds. *The Family Life Cycle: A Framework for Family Therapy*. New York: Gardner Press, 1980.

Chodorow, Nancy. *The Reproduction of Mothering: Psychoanalysis and the Sociology of Gender*. Berkeley and Los Angeles: University of California Press, 1978.

Clinebell, Charlotte. *Meet Me in the Middle: On Becoming Human Together*. New York: Harper & Row, 1973.

Clinebell, H. J. and C. H. *The Intimate Marriage*. New York: Harper & Row, 1970.

Cooper, David. *The Death of the Family*. New York: Pantheon Books, 1971.

De Rougement, Denis. *Love in the Western World*. Garden City, NY: Doubleday, 1957.

Ellison, Craig, ed. *Your Better Self: Christianity, Psychology and Self-Esteem*. San Francisco: Harper & Row, 1983.

Erikson, Erik. *Childhood and Society*. New York: Norton, 1963.

Evans, Donald. *Struggle and Fulfillment.* Toronto: Collins, 1979.

Fox, Matthew. *A Spirituality Named Compassion and the Healing of the Global Village, Humpty Dumpty and Us.* Minneapolis, MN: Winston Press, 1979.

_____. *Original Blessing.* Santa Fe, NM: Bear & Company, 1983.

Friday, Nancy. *My Mother, My Self.* New York: Dell, 1977.

Fromm, Eric. *The Art of Loving.* New York: Harper & Row, 1956.

Gilligan, Carol. *In a Different Voice.* Cambridge: Harvard University Press, 1982.

Goldberg, Herb. *The Hazards of Being Male.* New York: Signet Books, 1980.

Gould, Roger. *Transformations.* New York: Simon & Schuster, 1978.

Gratton, Carol. *Trusting.* New York: Crossroad, 1982.

Greene, Bernard L., ed. *The Psychotherapies of Marital Disharmony.* New York: The Free Press, 1965.

Greenwald, Jerry. *Creative Intimacy.* New York: Jove Publications, 1975.

Hoffman, Lynn. *Foundations of Family Therapy.* New York: Basic Books, 1981.

Jung, Carl. *Modern Man in Search of a Soul.* New York: Harcourt, Brace, 1933.

Kaplan, Louise. *Oneness and Separateness: From Infant to Individual.* New York: Simon & Schuster, 1978.

Keen, Sam. *The Passionate Life: Stages of Adult Loving.* San Francisco: Harper & Row, 1983.

Keleman, Stanley. *The Human Ground: Sexuality, Self and Survival.* Palo Alto, CA: Science and Behavior Books, 1975.

Kiersey, David, and Marilyn Bates. *Please Understand Me: Character and Temperament Types.* Del Mar, CA: Gnosology Books, 1984.

Kilpatrick, William. *Identity and Intimacy.* New York: Dell, 1975.

Krantzler, Mel. *Creative Divorce.* New York: Signet, 1973.

_____. *Creative Marriage.* New York: McGraw-Hill, 1981.

Kübler-Ross, Elizabeth. *On Death and Dying.* New York: Macmillan, 1970.

Laing, R. D. *Knots.* New York: Pantheon Books, 1970.

Lasch, Christopher. *The Minimal Self.* New York: Norton, 1984.

Lederer, William, and Donald Jackson. *The Mirages of Marriage.* New York: Norton, 1968.

Leech, Kenneth. *Soul Friend.* London: Sheldon Press, 1977.

Levinson, Daniel. *The Seasons of a Man's Life.* New York: Ballantine Books, 1978.

Loder, James E. *The Transforming Moment.* New York: Harper & Row, 1981.

Loevinger, Jane. *Ego Development.* San Francisco: Jossey-Bass, 1976.

Lowen, Alexander. *The Language of the Body.* New York: Collier-Macmillan, 1958.

_____. *Depression and the Body: The Biological Basis of Faith and Reality.* Balitmore: Penguin, 1973.

Mace, David and Vera. *How to Have a Happy Marriage.* Nashville, TN: Abingdon, 1977.

Mahler, Margaret, Fred Fine, and Anni Bergman. *The Psychological Birth of the Human Infant.* New York: Basic Books, 1975.

Masters, William, and Virginia Johnson. *The Pleasure Bond.* New York: Bantam Books, 1975.

May, Gerald. *Care of Mind Care of Spirit.* San Francisco: Harper & Row, 1982.

May, Rollo. *Love and Will.* New York: Norton, 1969.

Miller, Sherod, Elam Nunnally, and Daniel Wachman. *Talking Together.* Minneapolis, MN: Interpersonal Communications Programs, 1979.

Montagu, Ashley. *Touching.* New York: Columbia University Press, 1971.

Moustakos, Clark E. *Loneliness and Love.* Englewood Cliffs, NJ: Prentice-Hall, 1972.

Napier, A., and C. Whitaker. *The Family Crucible.* New York: Harper & Row, 1978.

Olsen, Paul. *Sons and Mothers: Why Men Behave as They Do.* New York: M Evans, 1981.

Olthuis, James H. *I Pledge You My Troth. A Christian View of Marriage, Family and Friendship.* San Francisco: Harper & Row, 1975.

Otto, Herbert, ed. *Marriage and Family Enrichment.* Nashville, TN: Abingdon, 1976.

Paolino, T., and B. McCrady, eds. *Marriage and Marital Therapy.* New York: Brunner/Mazel, 1978.

Paul, Jordan, and Margaret Paul. *Do I Have to Give Up Me to Be Loved by You?* Minneapolis, MN: Compcare Publications, 1983.

Peck, M. Scott. *The Road Less Travelled.* New York: Simon & Schuster, 1978.

Rogers, Carl B. *Becoming Partners.* New York: Dell, 1972.

Rubin, Lillian B. *Intimate Strangers.* San Francisco: Harper & Row, 1984.

———. *Women of a Certain Age.* New York: Basic Books, Harper Colophon, 1976.

Rubin, Theodore Isaac. *One to One.* New York: Viking Press, 1983.

Satir, Virginia. *Peoplemaking.* Palo Alto, CA: Science and Behavior Books, 1972.

Scarfe, Maggie. *Unfinished Business: Pressure Points in the Lives of Women.* Garden City, NY: Doubleday, 1980.

Shanahan, James Rue & Louise. *Daddy's Girl, Mama's Boy.* New York: Bobbs-Merrill, 1978.

Sheehy, Gail. *Passages.* New York: Bantam Books, 1976.

———. *Pathfinders.* New York: Bantam Books, 1981.

Smedes, Louis. *Sex for Christians.* Grand Rapids, MI: Eerdmans, 1976.

Tillich, Paul. *The Dynamics of Faith.* New York: Harper & Row, 1957.

Washbourne, Penelope. *Becoming Woman.* San Francisco: Harper & Row, 1977.

Whitehead, Evelyn and James. *Christian Life Patterns.* Garden City, NY: Doubleday, 1979.

Winnicott, D. W. *The Family and Individual Development.* London: Tavistock, 1965.
Wright, H. Norman. *Seasons of a Marriage.* Ventura, CA; Regal Books, 1982.